Praise for Switched-On Netw...

"*Switched-On-Networking* revolutionizes the ...
brain for success! Using Jerry and Donna's leadi ... ..., you can
get your mind lined up to optimize your existing network, as well as the
new connections you make. Networking can be more fun and easy than you
ever thought—and it can lead to surprising successes!"

Marci Shimoff, author of *Happy for No Reason*
and *Chicken Soup for the Woman's Soul*

"Wow! Easily switch on your ability to naturally, successfully and memorably
meet people with the breakthrough secrets in *Switched-On Networking.*
It's terrific!"

Dr. Joe Vitale, author of *Attract Money Now,*
star in *The Secret* movie

"Everyone can benefit from *Switched-On Networking.* The tools that
Jerry and Donna share in this book will enhance your success, prosperity
and bring more fun into your life."

Mark Victor Hansen, co-author of *Chicken Soup for the Soul* book series

"Confused about how to move your business to the next level? Empower
yourself with the life-enhancing tips in *Switched-On Networking* to
jump-start your business."

Suzanne E. Harrill, author of *The Harrill Solution:*
Secrets of Successful Relationships Revealed

"This book is a unique and powerful combination of the most leading-edge
networking and communication skills. The easy brain exercises in
Switched-On Networking will embed these techniques and skills
and replace the habits that are not serving you. Read and internalize the
concepts in this book and you will take your business, and your life, to a
whole new level."

Sara Pencil Blumenfeld, Personal Empowerment Coach and
author of *Nurturing Networker: Business Networking That Matters*

"Networking guru, Donna Fisher, and Brain Gym master, Dr. Jerry Teplitz, have joined forces to produce **Switched-On Networking,** an insight-filled guide to being a more successful networker—and more importantly, to becoming a more successful person. With practical steps for developing the ability to be confident in every networking opportunity, they make the whole process of building an active, empowering, productive network both fun and easy. No matter what you do in life, this book will make a powerful and positive difference in how you see yourself and everyone you meet."

Rob Pennington, Ph.D., Psychologist and author of
Find The Upside of the Down Times

"**Switched-On Networking** gives you the tools to networking your way to increased opportunities. Donna Fisher's concepts and Jerry Teplitz's easy processes lay out a blueprint for anyone interested in expanding their relationships that lead to more success … a must read."

Bob Frare, CSP, author of *PARTNER Selling*

"This networking book is a must-read for anyone who is hopeful of becoming an effective networker. It is chock-full of helpful advice and spiced with human relations principles that clearly and movingly describe networking as showing respect, dignity and courtesy toward connections you hope to build as mutually beneficial relationships."

Ken Marsh, author of *Fearless Networking!*

"In today's business environment, it is more important than ever that we utilize our networking skills to reach out and expand our sphere of contacts. **Switched-On Networking** is packed with tools and knowledge to enable you to do just that and more. This book is a must have!"

Germaine Porché, co-author, *Coach Anyone About Anything,*
Volumes 1 & 2

"**Switched-On Networking** gives a whole new approach to reprogramming your brain for success! This book gets your mind lined up for connecting and creating more and more opportunities with the people you meet."

Loral Langemeier, CEO/Founder of Live Out Loud,
international speaker, money expert and best-selling author
of the *Millionaire Maker 3* book series and *Put More Cash In Your Pocket*

"If you are on a mission to network with and serve vast numbers of amazing people across the world, and also desire to reap the rewards that come from providing a viable global service, then **Switched-On Networking** is an absolute must read! You can now stand on the shoulders of two pioneers in the fields of networking and brain optimization without having to experience the trials and tribulations of reinventing the wheel."

Dr. John Demartini, Founder of the Demartini Institute
and author of *The Breakthrough Experience:
The Revolutionary Approach to Personal Transformation*

"**Switched-On Networking** is 'State of the Art,' showing people how networking can become a way of life that leads to meaningful relationships. Donna and Jerry are the masters of making networking both FUN and fulfilling. This book is truly life's best prosperity tool."

Dan Valdez, founder of The Owners Alliance

"This book is unique in its ability to assist you in making a difference for the people in your network, feel good about who you are as a networker, and enhance your ability to accomplish fulfilling results."

Ron Sukenick, author of *The Power is in the Connection:
Taking Business Relationships to the Next Level*

"There are a lot of books that teach the techniques of networking. In **Switched-On Networking,** Donna Fisher and Dr. Jerry Teplitz teach us how to *become* a networker. The program they've developed helps us adopt the mindset that leads to true success in both our professional and personal lives. Only pick up this book if you are ready for success in both arenas!"

Greg Peters, founder of The Reluctant Networker, LLC

"**Switched-On-Networking** revolutionizes the idea of reprogramming your brain for success! Get your mind lined up for connecting and creating opportunities with the people you meet. If networking was an Olympic sport, Donna Fisher and Dr. Jerry Teplitz would win Gold Medals!"

Ruben Gonzalez, Olympian, Author, Keynote Speaker

"In their new book **Switched-On-Networking,** Donna Fisher and Dr. Jerry Teplitz combine networking fundamentals with cognitive calisthenics and give you a proven formula on how to create an empowered level of congruency in your relational networking. Focus on these fundamentals with a zest for supporting others—while raising your awareness for their business needs—and watch your networking skills soar!"

Bob Nicoll, author of *Remember the Ice and Other Paradigm Shifts* and *Exceptional Care for Your Valued Client*

"Donna has done it again! Collaborating with Dr. Jerry Teplitz, she highlights simple and powerful ideas that enhance quality of life and can be implemented immediately with ease and joy. The rewards are priceless! It's the little things that are the big things—this book is filled with treasures. Thank you!"

Robin Blanc Mascari, Co-founder of EnlightenedNetworking.com

"This is a must-read book for anyone who is looking for a job or who anticipates looking for a better job in the future. The number one source of great employees comes from referrals, so the bigger and better your network is the better the chance you will be referred to that dream job. *Switched-On-Networking* is packed with real take home practical tools, tips and techniques that you can apply immediately. So start building your network today."

Mel Kleiman, President, Humetrics

"The concept of **Switched-On Networking** is one of the most powerful networking tools I've encountered. Teplitz and Fisher's blend of scientific research and networking expertise has produced a guide for networking success that is in a league of its own."

Ivan Misner, Ph.D., *NY Times* Bestselling Author and Founder of BNI®

SWITCHED-ON
NETWORKING

BALANCE YOUR BRAIN
FOR NETWORKING SUCCESS

JERRY V. TEPLITZ, J.D., PH.D.
AND DONNA FISHER

WITH NORMA ECKROATE

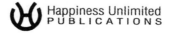
Happiness Unlimited
PUBLICATIONS

Happiness Unlimited Publications
1304 Woodhurst Drive
Virginia Beach, VA 23454

Library of Congress Publisher's Cataloging-in-Publication Data
Teplitz, Jerry.
Switched-on networking : balance your brain for
networking success / Jerry V. Teplitz and Donna Fisher ;
with Norma Eckroate.
    p. cm.
  ISBN: 978-0-939372-23-2
  1. Interpersonal communication. 2. Mind and body. 3.
Success in business.   I. Fisher, Donna. II. Eckroate,
Norma. III. Title.
BF161 .T26 2011
650.1—dc22
Library of Congress Control Number: 2011910677

Printed in the United States of America.
15 14 13 12 11 10 9 8 7 6 5 4 3 2 1

Cover Design by Daniel Yaeger
Book Design by Lynn Snyder
Illustrations by Cris Arbo
Photographs by Elizabeth Balcar
This book is available at quantity discounts for bulk purchases.

For information, please call 800 77-RELAX

Website: www.Teplitz.com   www.DonnaFisher.com

Free Online Videos

To assist you with the processes described in this book, online video demos are available at www.SwitchedOnNetworking.com/demo. On these videos you will learn ways to access your own internal biofeedback responses to tell you if your body is switched off or switched on to certain stimuli. We'll also give you this link at the appropriate sections in the book in case you want to wait and watch the videos at that time—or watch them again at that time.

Also, to view demo videos on Donna and Jerry's trainings and presentations, go to:

www.Teplitz.com/media/keynote/keynote1.html

and

www.youtube.com/DonnaFisher1

CONTENTS

INTRODUCTION

Have you ever wondered why some people make amazing connections through networking, while others just can't seem to get the hang of it? Are successful networkers simply more congenial or more intelligent? Do they start out with connections to more powerful centers of influence? Do they just innately have better communication skills? Or is something else going on? Successful networkers not only have great communication skills and proven follow-up systems, they also have an elusive quality that we might call the X-factor. This X-factor includes an expanded awareness, an ability to empower oneself, and a strong knack to connect with people.

Successful networkers communicate with others easily. They enjoy the process of connecting with people and have mentally trained themselves to "think as a resource" in order to efficiently accomplish goals. For effective networkers, setbacks are not failures; they are simply opportunities to continue to network to find the appropriate resources. Successful networkers enjoy the "treasure hunt" for the "jewels" that lead to the fulfillment of their own goals, as well as the goals of others in their network. Whether they know it or not, they are successful because they have subconscious beliefs that support their success.

If you're like most people, you have subconscious beliefs that *do not* support success. For example, if you have thoughts like, "People never respond to my requests," then it's more likely that your requests will go unanswered. If you believe that asking for a referral is hard, it will be more difficult to expand your network. Any limiting or negative beliefs that you hold about success, abundance, effectiveness, or other issues relating to networking are part of your subconscious programming and, when you are faced with situations relating to these topics, they automatically kick in.

The big question, though, is this: Where does that negative programming come from? Why do you automatically "default" to the little voice inside that says that people don't respond positively to you? Why doesn't your little inner voice shout out to you: *"I can do this!"* *"Meeting new business prospects is easy!"* *"I'm very comfortable and confident when it comes time to meet new people!"*

The problem is that the programming in your subconscious mind is locked in there—like a database of stored programs on a computer. In his book *Biology of Belief,* Dr. Bruce Lipton explains[1]:

...the subconscious mind is a repository of stimulus-response tapes derived from instincts and learned experiences. The subconscious mind is strictly habitual; it will play the same behavioral responses to life's signals over and over again, much to our chagrin. How many times have you found yourself going ballistic over something trivial like an open toothpaste tube? You have been trained since childhood to carefully replace the cap. When you find the tube with its cap left off, your "buttons are pushed" and you automatically fly into a rage. You've just experienced the simple stimulus-response of a behavior program stored in the subconscious mind.

When it comes to sheer neurological processing abilities, the subconscious mind is millions of times more powerful than the conscious mind. If the desires of the conscious mind conflict with the programs in the subconscious mind, which 'mind' do you think will win over? You can repeat the positive affirmation that you are lovable over and over or that your cancer tumor will shrink. But if, as a child, you heard over and over that you are worthless and sickly, those messages programmed in your subconscious mind will undermine your best conscious efforts to change your life.

---

1   Lipton, Bruce H., Ph.D., *The Biology of Belief,* Hay House, 2008, pages 97-98.

Lipton further explains that the *subconscious mind* is like an "autopilot" that processes up to 20,000,000 environmental stimuli per second while the *conscious mind* is a manual control that can process only about forty environmental stimuli per second. Therefore, the subconscious mind, with its speed and efficiency, is basically "auto-piloting" our lives. In most cases, those areas of our lives that are successful continue to be successful because our subconscious beliefs support that success. Those areas that are stressful and challenging continue to stress and challenge us because, likewise, we have subconscious beliefs that keep the status quo in place in those areas.

Many of today's motivational experts explain the same concept in a different way. Some refer to it as the Law of Attraction and tell us that we are attracting everything in our lives, even that which we say "no" to. They say the trick is to focus on what we *want,* not what we *don't want.* However, that's only part of the picture. If will power, commitment, and positive thinking were enough to override limiting beliefs that are programmed in our subconscious, this world would be brimming over with successful, happy people.

You may have read many books on networking and you've probably attended numerous business seminars. You might even have a business coach or mentor. But the success you're striving for may still be elusive as long as your subconscious mind is running old programming that blocks or limits you. The fact is that most experts don't tell you *how* to change that default setting in your subconscious so it will "default" into positive thinking.

A study published in 2010 in *Psychological Science* found that if people believed in positive affirmations, saying them over and over again would work for the person. If the person who was saying the affirmation over and over again had low self-esteem, then saying the positive affirmation would make the person feel worse.[2] So who wants to feel worse when you are doing something that is supposed to be

---

2   Wood, J.V., Perunovie, E., & Lee, J.W. (2009). Positive Self-Statements: Power for Some, Peril for Others. *Psychological Science,* 20, 860-865

positive for you? The likelihood is that the person would stop saying the affirmations and simply give up.

There is good news here; there are ways to reprogram the hard drive of our subconscious so we can attain the success we want. This book presents an interactive experience that will "switch you on" for success at networking through a brain optimization process that reprograms and changes your old subconscious programming. It brings together the best of the work of two powerhouse pioneers, Donna Fisher, and Jerry Teplitz, JD, PhD, who have dedicated their careers to helping others attain mastery in their lives through keynotes, seminars, books and coaching.

Donna Fisher, known as an expert in networking and communication skills, has authored four books, which have been translated into five foreign languages, and has taught thousands of people how to be effective networkers. Donna's strategies and tips inspire people to build a strong network of support that enhances their lives personally and professionally.

Dr. Jerry Teplitz, known as "an expert in Brain Performance Optimization," has spent more than three decades teaching revolutionary techniques that quite literally switch-on the body and the mind to achieve full potential through optimum brain performance by using movement exercises called Brain Gym®.

Switched-On Networking is part of a series of "Switched-On" books and seminars that includes subjects such as sales, network marketing, and management that have catapulted participants into phenomenal growth. These books and seminars are so different, so unique, and so powerful that they are recommended by other master trainers who have their own training programs. In this book, you will learn to create new wiring around your subconscious beliefs that will literally redirect your conscious behavior so you can easily and quickly empower yourself to be and do your best in every networking situation. The Brain Gym processes that Jerry leads you through will enable you to fully utilize the great networking strategies that Donna shares.

Switched-On Networking will assist you in fully utilizing the communication skills you have learned in the past—and it doesn't conflict with any other technique-oriented training seminars you have already learned or any networking trainings you take in the future. As Andy Miller, trainer for the Sandler Training Institute of Virginia said about Jerry's Switched-On Selling seminar "Jerry, you have found the missing piece! This should be a required seminar before anyone pursues traditional sales training," You'll find the same thing holds true for *Switched-On Networking*.

The Brain Gym® process that you will learn in this book was created by Paul E. Dennison, PhD and Gail E. Dennison.[3] Through a series of movements, exercises, and a process called a Balance, Brain Gym movements will literally reprogram your subconscious beliefs. To use a computer analogy, you will first identify an old belief that isn't serving you. Then you will hit the delete key to release that belief, replace it with a new empowering belief, and, finally, click on "save" to store that new belief permanently in the subconscious mind.

The Brain Gym process allows you to easily identify and overcome your fears. Fear has a powerful effect on a person's behavior; it can explain the difference between success and failure in business. When a person is functioning out of fear—for instance, fear of rejection—he will attempt to avoid the cause of the fear. If you are afraid of rejection, you may hesitate to network by making calls or approaching people, even people who are interested in your product or service. As a result, you will have mediocre business or personal success.

What kind of benefits can you expect from experiencing the Switched-On Networking approach? To help you understand the benefits, let's examine for a moment the research Jerry conducted on the effectiveness of the *Switched-On Selling* seminar with 695 attendees. At the beginning of the seminar, he asked participants to complete a 20-item questionnaire that rated their attitudes, their perception of themselves, and their effectiveness in the selling process. The question-naire was comprised of a series of statements about making a presenta-

---

3 The Brain Gym® movements and exercises used in this publication are used with the permission of Brain Gym International but the application of these movements does not necessarily reflect the educational philosophy of Brain Gym® International or the Brain Gym authors, Paul and Gail Dennison, California, USA.

tion to a prospect, such as, "I handle rejection well" and "I am comfortable asking for the order." The participants were asked to indicate their attitude about each statement, with response choices of "strongly agree," "agree," "disagree," and "strongly disagree."

At the end of the day, they completed the same questionnaire again to determine the immediate impact of the seminar. A follow up was done a month later when they were asked to complete the questionnaire a third time to determine if the improvement they experienced at the seminar had translated to real-life experience. The follow-up questionnaire was also designed to help determine if the participants had initially overrated the seminar's impact due to the placebo effect or a seminar "high."

The results were remarkable. Here's an example. When responding to the statement, *I am comfortable asking for the order and closing the sale* at the beginning of the seminar, 52 percent of the participants admitted that asking for the order and closing the sale was a problem for them. Only 16 percent said they handled asking for the order and closing the sale well.

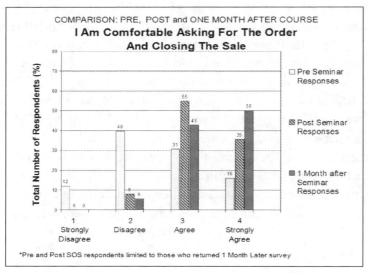

At the end of the seminar, 55 percent of the respondents answered "Well" to asking for the order and closing the sales and 35 percent said

"Very Well," while only 8 percent were left saying they still felt it was a problem for them. So during this one-day seminar, something happened to 90 percent of the attendees, who no longer felt uncomfortable asking for the order and closing the sale.

Of course, those responses were given in a vacuum—while the participants were still at the seminar. It was great that they left with the strong feeling that they could now ask for the order and close the sale, but the proof is in the pudding. How would this translate in the real world of daily sales calls? That's why the follow-up questionnaire one month after the seminar was so important. An amazing 50 percent of the individuals who responded to the follow-up questionnaire said they felt they could ask for the order and close the sale very well. This was a jump of 34 percent from the pre-seminar results. Only 6 percent of the respondents still felt it was still a problem for them to ask for the order and close the sale.

A statistician analyzed the results on all the questions and reported that the likelihood of such a rate of improvement was at the .0001 level of probability of occurring. For those of you who are not statisticians, this means the seminar had an extraordinarily beneficial impact on the perceptions of the participants. (A Summary of the study can be found in Appendix B. The full study is available at www.Teplitz.com.)

These studies show that the seminar empowered participants in numerous aspects of selling, including handling rejection and asking for referrals, while releasing fears, worries, and concerns. Almost everyone who participated became switched-on to selling, yet they did it without learning a single new sales technique.

What made these remarkable results possible? These individuals simply attended the seminar, participated in the process, and walked out "switched-on." This book takes you through similar processes that relate specifically to networking. So, in this book, you've got it all. Jerry's mind-body re-wiring approach is matched with the techniques and strategies of Donna Fisher, who is one of the world's foremost networking gurus, giving you tools to reach levels of success that you may not have thought possible.

When you complete this book, you will find that:
- What you are already doing as a networker, you will do even better;
- What you would like to do better when networking, you will easily improve; and
- What you are avoiding doing, you will be able to do.

Switched-On Networking is about changing your mind. Literally. If you have ever felt nervous before walking into a networking event, or felt hesitant to ask for support, or were uncertain about how to effectively introduce yourself to others, be prepared for some life-changing synergy as you learn how to re-educate your brain using your body with the Brain Gym movements and, at the same time, integrate the expertise of Donna's proven techniques and strategies into your life as a networker.

Since you will be learning some unique techniques in this book, you may find it helpful to view our online video demonstrations at www.SwitchedOnNetworking.com/demo. (If you want to wait to view the videos until this material is covered in the chapters, we will also provide the link in the relevant sections.)

A Few Words from Donna

Switched-On Networking offers a unique combination of solid networking skills and strategies coupled with the exciting breakthrough of the Brain Gym movements, creating a unique, one-of-a-kind experience for any reader. Think about it. There is no other, singular approach anywhere in the world that offers this dual track for people in such a meaningful and powerful way—my approach to networking and Jerry's approach to balancing your brain present a unique approach for greater success in your business.

Switched-On Networking utilizes brain optimization technology for all of the aspects of networking, including having a positive attitude about networking, fulfilling your networking goals, having effective people skills, nurturing your existing network, connecting online and face-to-face, upgrading your conversation skills when networking, using networking as a time-saver, and being a prosperous networker. For example, let's look at mingling at a networking event. Since you never know who you are going to meet and how they are going to respond to you, you might feel a little nervous when you walk in to that event. Some people will avoid the discomfort of meeting new people by immediately finding someone they know to talk with. Being an effective networker requires developing the confidence to comfortably approach people, put people at ease, and generate interesting conversation.

The stress of meeting new people can cause some people to simply avoid going to a networking event. Some people will go to the event but then "hide out" in safe conversations where they don't have to meet new people. And others will approach people with such nervousness that a connection never happens and they confirm for themselves that networking does not work for them. In networking scenarios, the ability to confidently communicate and connect with people can make the difference so that magical synchronicities show up in your life.

The brain integration techniques in *Switched-On Networking* will allow you to immediately move past these types of mental and/or physical blocks that you might encounter in the process of networking. Once you have gone through this process, your brain will be switched-on—and that will allow you to fully incorporate and utilize my networking perspectives. This combination of leading-edge mind-body technology with leading-edge networking skills gives you everything you need to be effective in any networking scenario.

A Few Words from Jerry

The Brain Gym process you'll learn in this book will easily enable you to remove the mental blocks you experience in any part of the networking process. This process allows you to re-format your mental programming and activate new neural pathways so you can balance your brain in new ways.

Did you know that the stem cells in your body manufacture 10,000 new brain cells every day? Scientists use the term neuroplasticity to describe the ability of the brain to develop new neuronal and synaptic connections and thereby re-wire itself. It was once believed that only children's brains had this capacity but now we know that adult's brains can also be re-wired or redeveloped. And that's what we're doing with Brain Gym. Through a series of easy movements and exercises, you can simply and easily re-wire and create new balance in the circuitry of your brain to generate these new neural pathways to enhance performance in all areas of your life, including intellectual, creative, athletic, and interpersonal, and of course, in the case of this book, networking. As I mentioned earlier, it's as if you are clicking on "delete" to release the old belief, hitting "replace" to install the new belief, and then clicking "save" to store that new belief. And you wind up with a new balance in your brain.

For over three decades, I've researched the Brain Gym approach in various arenas of business. From my own studies, the research that our corporate clients have done, and the stories that graduates have shared, I can say with total confidence that this *Switched-On Networking* book will allow you to experience amazing changes in your networking abilities.

Our Challenge to You

We know it's likely that you've already put lots of time and effort into developing your networking skill sets. We're not suggesting that you start over. But we are suggesting that you re-wire and rebalance your brain's programming to more fully utilize and optimize what you have learned in the past by using this book as an interactive tool. Perhaps you feel you've really mastered some aspects of networking. While you have the choice of skipping ahead to another section of the book, we're suggesting that you don't do that. If you are very experienced in networking, then the best way to use this book is to look at it as a refresher course. The tools Jerry presents using Brain Gym give you the opportunity at the end of each chapter the ability to move into "re-wiring and rebalancing mode."

If you are new to networking, this book will get you over your blocks even before you experience them. As you learn the techniques from Donna, you'll simply be saying to yourself, "I can do that," "That's a piece of cake," "That's easy." Like others who have used this simple tool, you will quickly move to seeing immediate demonstrations of success where it counts—in your real world experiences.

As you do the Brain Gym exercises in this book, it is crucial that you actively participate in order to go beyond your intellectual under-standing of Donna's networking strategies. *Switched-On Networking* is not about having an intellectual understanding of something; it is about re-wiring and rebalancing your brain to release the mental and physical blockages that are holding you back from the level of success you desire.

Here's how the book is divided:

- In Part I, Jerry explains Brain Gym and how it is used in *Switched-On Networking.* He also presents descriptions and explanations of all of the Brain Gym Movements and Exercises that you will perform in the Balances in Part II.

- Part II is divided into the various aspects of networking—fulfilling your networking goals, having effective people skills, nurturing your existing network, connecting online and face-to-face, upgrading your conversation skills when networking, using networking as a time-saver, and being a prosperous net-worker. In each of these chapters, Donna shares her networking success strategies. Then, at the end of each chapter, Jerry takes you through the Brain Gym process, ending with a Balance[4] to switch you on for the aspects of networking that you specifically want to make more effective and successful.

- In Part III, Jerry will show you how to continue to reinforce the rebalancing you have done and how to set your energy and focus every day by using the Brain Gym movements and exercises.

So sit back, relax, and participate, as you are now about to experience the life-changing power of *Switched-On Networking.* Enjoy the journey!

---

4   The *Switched-On Networking* Balances are designed differently from the way Brain Gym Balances are taught in the Brain Gym Courses.

PART I

Brain Optimization™—Re-Wiring & Rebalancing Your Brain for Networking Success

BY JERRY V. TEPLITZ, J.D., PH.D.

CHAPTER 1

WHAT IS BRAIN OPTIMIZATION?

In Switched-On Networking, a process called Brain Gym literally optimizes your mind-body system by re-educating it and rebalancing it so you can accomplish most skills or functions with greater ease and efficiency. Specific Brain Gym movements and exercises are used to activate different parts of the brain for optimal storage, retrieval, and processing of information. The goal is to integrate the whole brain for optimal functioning by reprogramming any areas in which your beliefs are blocking the achievement of your goals.

Brain Gym was originally developed by Dr. Paul Dennison and Gail Dennison. Dr. Dennison is an educator and researcher who originally worked with children and adults with learning challenges and/or difficulties with motor coordination skills. Dennison discovered that these problems were caused by a lack of coordination among the different parts of the brain and body; therefore, he sought innovative ways to use the mind-body connection to help these individuals learn easier and more effectively.

After fifteen years of research, Dr. Dennison combined the techniques used in Applied Kinesiology and Neural Optometry, as well as research in the fields of movement, education and child development theory, into a unique system of learning and brain re-patterning that creates new neural wiring in the brain. As his work continued, Dr. Dennison also developed methods to integrate other parts of the brain for a "whole brain" integration that includes the left and right hemispheres, the top and bottom, and the front and back of the brain. Dr. Dennison began this work in 1969 and today thousands of practitioners and instructors facilitate Brain Gym programs in classrooms, businesses, and homes around the world.

In case you read that last paragraph quickly, let me restate the one idea that is of primary importance to an understanding of Brain Gym—it is designed to integrate the different parts of the brain. *It does this by creating new neural wiring in the brain, which rebalances the brain for optimum success.* In this book, you will frequently see the words "re-wiring" and "re-educating" and "rebalancing." This is literally what Brain Gym does. It allows you to release old thought patterns that negatively impact the way you function in the world and re-wire the neural pathways to allow for re-education and rebalancing. This process creates new reactions and new pathways in a positive vein. If this sounds like a big claim, you'll have the opportunity to read the research and experience it for yourself as you do the Brain Gym exercises. So read on. Let the evidence and your experience of your own re-educated neural wiring become the real proof of the power of this work.

I first became aware of Brain Gym one day while I was waiting for a flight in an airport after teaching a seminar. A man introduced himself to me and said that he had been at one of my business seminars several years earlier and found the material I presented called Behavioral Kinesiology very impactful. He told me that my seminar opened him up to further explorations and he was now studying a new method of brain integration called Brain Gym. He showed me how to do some of the movements involved with this process and I was immediately impressed. The process made my body feel relaxed in the midst of a bustling airport and I even had an appreciable energy boost. I was interested!

At the time, Brain Gym was taught under the banner of Educational Kinesiology, also known as "Edu-K." I signed up for the first three-day Edu-K class[5] and quickly realized the profound implication of the process when applied to business. As I mentioned, the Brain Gym movements were originally developed to assist those with learning challenges. However, in the past few decades Brain Gym has been

---

5   Information on Brain Gym classes can be obtained by contacting Brain Gym International at
     www.braingym.org.

adapted to many other arenas for both children and adults, including regular classroom settings where it has led to significant improvements for students in subjects such as reading, spelling, math, handwriting, and test-taking. Students who use Brain Gym movements also experience improvements in comprehension, concentration, communication, memory, organizational skills, performance skills, and overcoming hyperactivity

Brain Gym movements and exercises bring neurological efficiency to your brain, enhancing your body's innate intelligence and quickly replacing old patterns of negative reactions and emotions with positive emotions and responses. This is the key—this system not only makes your brain more efficient, it also allows you to get rid of negative programming.

Carla Hannaford, author of *Smart Moves: Why Learning is Not All in Your Head,* states that Brain Gym, as well as other movements like walking, dancing, skipping, twirling, Tai Chi, Yoga, and even the rough and tumble play of children, appear to cause adjustments that assist the brain in the learning process. Dee Coulter, a cognitive specialist and neuroscience educator quoted in Hannaford's book, calls these adjustments "micro-interventions." She explains that these adjustments bring about major change because they supply the necessary integration and also reverse the expectation of failure.[6]

Brain Gym simply enhances the body's abilities to do what it does naturally. These movements and exercises can create the opportunity for greater networking success than you have ever imagined and they can also be used to enhance memory, learning, physical coordination, and the achievement of your life goals.

I saw applications for this work in the business world and received permission to expand Brain Gym in that direction in 1986 by creating my first Switched-On seminar, Switched-On Selling. I also coauthored the book *Brain Gym for Business: Instant Brain Boosters for On-The-Job Success* with Dr. Dennison and Gail Dennison.

---

6   Hannaford, Carla. *Smart Moves: Why Learning Is Not All In Your Head.* 1995. Salt Lake City, Utah: Great River Books, 2005, page 110.

Why the Brain Switches Off

Certain areas of your brain are filled with patterns and programming that are "locked" in. These patterns and programs control your thoughts, your reactions, your interactions with others, your ability to effectively apply networking skills, and even your ability to be spontaneous. If this programming has negative messages locked in, then no matter how many networking techniques you learn or how much effort you put into making changes, your success may be difficult and limited.

The programming that is locked into your brain comes from many sources, including your DNA. It is also has developed from the four pillars of your youth—your parents, your peers, your school, and your culture. If you were repeatedly exposed to the idea that you weren't "good" enough or smart enough; that only "lucky" people are successful; that your sex, the color of your skin, your ethnic background, or your height, weight, or age restrict your chances in life; or any one of thousands of other negative, self-limiting beliefs, you have probably incorporated those beliefs into your life and are unconsciously living out those messages every day. Most people aren't even consciously aware of the extent to which limited thinking is wired into their brain. In many cases, these messages feed your "self talk"—the chatter that goes on in your head—constantly reinforcing the "I'm not good enough" messages. All you need to do is look at your life to know if that is the case for you. Simply ask yourself: *Do I have what I want—or does success seem difficult and elusive?*

When your brain is "switched-off" to certain aspects of networking, it is a struggle to perform them. As I mentioned earlier, a person getting ready to make a call and then suddenly decides instead to clean their desk or organize their files—anything to avoid making the call has a block. The idea of making the call is switching off the person's brain. And when the brain switches off, it becomes such a struggle to perform the task at hand that the easiest thing to do is to avoid it by doing something else. If you have to do the task, you do it poorly.

The brain can also switch off to certain activities due to a built-in survival mechanism. To understand how this works, we have to look at the amygdala, a part of the brain that we inherited from our primitive ancestors. Located deep within the medial temporal lobes of the brain, this almond-shaped group of neurons perform a primary role in the memory as it relates to processing emotional reactions. The amygdala is triggered whenever a threatening situation arises, initiating the "fight, freeze, or flight" response in the body and basically overriding the "rational" part of the brain.

Psychologist Daniel Goleman refers to the amygdala as "the specialist for emotional matters."[7] In his book, *Emotional Intelligence,* Goleman explains that it is this area of the brain that gauges the emotional significance of events. He shares the story of a young man whose amygdala was surgically removed to control seizures. After the surgery, the young man became totally disinterested in people and preferred no human contact. With no amygdala, he seemed to have no feelings at all.

The amygdala is wired to analyze every experience we have to determine if trouble looms. Goleman explains[8]:

This puts the amygdala in a powerful post in mental life, something like a psychological sentinel, challenging every situation, every perception, with but one kind of question in mind, the most primitive: "Is this something I hate? That hurts me? Something I fear?" If so—if the external event that you are experiencing draws a "Yes"—the amygdala reacts instantaneously, like a neural tripwire, telegraphing a message of crisis to all parts of the brain. In the brain's architecture, the amygdala is poised something like an alarm company where operators stand ready to send out emergency calls to the fire department, police, and a neighbor whenever a home security system signals trouble. When it sounds an alarm of say, fear, it sends urgent messages to every major part of the brain: it triggers the secretion of the body's fight-or-flight hormones, which mobilizes the centers for movement, and activates the cardiovascular system, the muscles, and the gut.

---

7   Goleman, Daniel, Ph.D., *Emotional Intelligence,* Bantam Books, 1995, page 15.
8   Goleman, Daniel, Ph.D., page 16.

To the extent that the amygdala takes over during an emotional emergency, the rational part of the brain doesn't have a chance to control what's going on. This rational part, which governs choice, is in the part of the brain called the cerebrum, which developed much later in the evolution of the human brain. An example of the amygdala-in-action is a news story about an out-of-control van that careened into three women pedestrians, striking all three. A number of bystanders reacted by rushing to the van, pulling the driver and passenger from their vehicle, and beating them to death. Seven men were charged with the murder of the driver and his passenger. It turned out that the accident was not even due to driver error. Of course, whether the driver was in error or not, the mob reaction had no justification. This type of deadly group reaction can be the result of emotional hijacking of the brain by the portion of the amygdala that triggered the adrenaline response. There are numerous news stories of people reacting first, thinking second. The amygdala takes charge and otherwise-sane people sometimes respond insanely.

So how can we control which part of the brain is in charge? Let's look at a common activity that is difficult for some people, such as driving on the freeway, and see how the brain processes the information. A person who is challenged by freeway driving doesn't even have to be behind the wheel to have a reaction to it. All he has to do is *think* about driving on the freeway for his brain to be triggered. As soon as the brain is presented with the thought of freeway driving, it quickly reviews the situation to determine if there are any past situations that relate to this thought. Keep in mind that we're talking about a *thought* and not the actual act of driving on the freeway. The situation from the past may be a time in his childhood when he was in an accident or saw an accident on the freeway. The fear feeling he has now about driving on freeways is caused by this past event "kicking in." He doesn't have a choice about how to act in the matter because situations in his past have wired his emotional circuitry to respond with fear. He is switched off to freeway driving.

Fear is a powerful force that can stop us from achieving what we want. Thoughts that a networker might have such as "What if I can't successfully connect with people?" "What if I get rejected?" and

"What will people say?" may be occurring at both the conscious and unconscious level. These fears will keep you stuck as they influence your thoughts, attitudes, and even the level of enthusiasm you project when you are networking. The Brain Gym movements can eliminate and release these fears and, at the same time, re-educate the brain and body to prefer a positive pattern so you are able to achieve the success you desire.

Brain Gym in Other Arenas

As explained earlier, Brain Gym can be used in many different arenas of our personal life and work life, including education and sports. The success of the original Switched-On Selling seminar led me to adapt it into a seminar for managers called Switched-On Management and another for network marketers called Switched-On Network Marketing. Now, the sky's the limit with the potential for Switched-On seminars and books that assist individuals in switching-on their lives for a myriad of personal and professional issues.

In addition to creating the seminars I mentioned above, I also assisted Pamela Curlee in the creation of her original manual for a golf seminar called Switched-On Golf"®. Pamela's physician husband, Paul, was a mediocre golfer before taking the seminar. Afterwards he became the proud winner of four golf tournaments and dropped his handicap from 18 to 10. Another Switched-On Golf attendee was a golf instructor who reported that the first time he played after taking the seminar he hit a hole-in-one. Impressed by his own success with Brain Gym, he incorporated the Brain Gym movements into his students' golf lessons. In the first summer that he did this, three of his thirty students hit holes-in-one! Ask any golfer and they'll tell you these numbers are simply amazing.

In addition to helping Pamela create the original Switched-On Golf seminar, I've also created a DVD called *Par and Beyond: Secrets to Better Golf* that demonstrates many more brain integration methods that I've developed from Behavioral Kinesiology. A typical response to this DVD is contained in a letter I received from Shep Hyken after he put the methods into practice. He writes:

Within a week of watching the video my scores started dropping two to four strokes each round. I was finding that my drives were going longer and more in play than usual... I was a 16 handicap just a month ago. I've been hovering around 15-16 for the last several years. Since watching the program, I've dropped to a 14 and according to the computer I'm trending to a 12! And I don't even practice! More pars seem to be the norm. And just ten days ago I shot the best round ever at my home course—a 76! Your video program allows me to concentrate and focus like I've never done before... It works!

Here's a response to the *Par and Beyond DVD* from Tom Fox, writer for *Travel and Leisure Golf* magazine:
I was ready to throw my clubs in the nearest water hazard because the game had stopped being fun for me. It's easy to obsess about swing thoughts and mental checklists, which are all about what to think about. *Par and Beyond* focuses on *how* to think and the difference shows up on the scorecard and in congratulations from your playing partners. Jerry's techniques improved my game, but more important, reminded me how to have fun playing a game I love.

For more information, visit my website at www.Golf-Help.info.

The Brain Switch:
Balancing the Brain's Hemispheres

To understand Brain Gym, we need to briefly explore the way the brain works so you'll see how it applies to networking. It's important to note that, for the purposes of this book, I am presenting a rather simplified model of brain functioning by focusing on the left hemisphere and right hemispheres of the cerebral cortex. Although science now concludes that there are no absolutes when it comes to brain organization, generally the left brain is the logical, analytical side of the brain and the right brain is the gestalt or "big picture" part of the brain.

Let's start with the *left hemisphere.* Besides being the logical hemisphere, the left hemisphere takes the lead for skills such as language and arithmetic. It processes information piece by piece, logically, analytically, and in a sequential manner. The left hemisphere also generally controls physical movement on the right side of our body. The *right hemisphere* is primarily the reflex or gestalt hemisphere. It has the ability to see the whole picture rather than focusing on the individual pieces. It is the receptive side of the brain and it absorbs and stores information gathered by the senses. The right hemisphere controls physical movement on the left side of our body. Again, remember that we're generalizing here and exceptions to this model of the functions of the two hemispheres exist; however, this model is accepted as the way most of us are "wired."

When the two hemispheres are integrated and balanced, they cooperate and communicate with each other, giving us the ability to function smoothly in our daily lives. Messages are constantly transmitted as electrical and chemical signals through the nervous system, the circulatory system to the brain, and throughout the body. For example, when you want to turn on a light switch, you first have the thought that the light is off and needs to be turned on. To accomplish this task you walk across the room, raise your hand to the switch, and flip the switch with your fingers. A coordination of movements in both the left and right hemispheres is necessary for even this simple action to be carried out. If your hemispheres weren't integrated and communicating, you might end up stumbling over a piece of furniture, putting a hole in the wall, or going out the door instead of turning on the light.

So how does this relate to networking? A lack of brain coordination can result in a host of difficulties and challenges, such as:

- Feeling awkward and uncomfortable when attending networking events.
- Difficulty connecting with people to build strong networking relationships.
- Frustration over not producing the results you desire when networking.
- Feeling uncomfortable making requests for fear of appearing weak and needy.

- Difficulty balancing how much time to spend with online and face-to-face networking.
- Feeling ineffective at creating productive conversations in networking situations.
- Inability to speak clearly about what you do in order to connect with the best resources.
- "Dropping the ball" on referrals and follow up.
- Allowing either shyness or aggressiveness to be a "roadblock" for creating a strong network of support.

When you function primarily out of either the left or the right side of the brain you are functioning "homolaterally," which means one-sided functioning. An example of this is found in our school systems. The education system in the U.S. features an analytic approach, causing an over-emphasis on left hemisphere dominance. To succeed in this learning environment, students need to focus on being more left-brain dominant because most of their daily tasks do not involve the right hemisphere. The result is that children who are predominately right hemisphere wired struggle to succeed.

The left and right hemispheres of the brain communicate with each other via the corpus callosum, the membrane that divides the two hemispheres. In a baby, there are 200 million nerve fibers that run across the corpus callosum connecting the hemispheres. It can be compared to a superhighway that allows messages to go back and forth between the two hemispheres, sending reactions and thoughts in the form of electrochemical impulses. The brain contains an estimated one quadrillion nerve connections. But as we get older and continually emphasize one hemisphere over the other, many of these connections begin to atrophy. Therefore, as most people age, there are fewer connections available, which means fewer messages are going across the corpus callosum. This makes it even more challenging to use the "whole" brain and we end up with a "one-brained" or homolateral approach to life, with only one side of the brain firing at a time. For this reason, performing right-hemispheric functions, as well as functions that require both hemispheres to operate together, becomes more difficult for many people.

The learning challenges that result cause us to develop compensating mechanisms to survive in the world. For example, a student might instinctively begin to sit on the far left side of a classroom because he can better understand what is being written on the chalkboard or comprehend what the teacher is saying from the left side of the room. Even though he is not aware of the reasons behind it, this is the way he compensates for the lack of integration between the hemispheres. These compensating mechanisms allow the person to perform an activity with greater success, but there is a price to pay because it is still generally more difficult and takes longer to do the task. And that is especially true if he has no choice but to sit on the "wrong" side of the room. While the learning challenges faced by the average person aren't as exaggerated as those with attention deficit disorder or dyslexia, they do have an impact on the way we function and on our success in the world.

Over 10,000 brain cells are manufactured in your body every single day. And these brain cells have a built-in "plasticity," or ability to evolve. Brain Gym allows us to utilize this neuroplasticity and stimulate the brain, creating more branching neural pathways. But when brain stimulation stops, so does the branching. According to Carla Hannaford[9]:

> These pathways alter from moment to moment in our lives. Ultimately they form only a few permanent connections at the synapses with particular target cells. Experience can further modify these synapses as well. Many synaptic connections are made as new learning occurs. Later, these linkages are pared down in a specific way that increases efficiency of thought. Neurons may have anywhere from 1,000 to 10,000 synapses and may receive information from 1,000 other neurons. Neurons with the most connections, an average of 300,000, are located in the cerebellum, the primary movement center of the brain, again pointing to the importance of movement and experience to learning.

---

9   Hannaford, page 24.

Brain Gym gives us the ability to release old patterns so we can learn with less stress and develop more confidence. It enhances our ability to access our natural creativity by using more of our mental and physical potential. The movements also assist in clearing emotional stress that can affect us both mentally and physically. Reported benefits include improvements in such areas as vision, listening, learning, memory, self-expression, and coordination in children and adults. Teachers typically report improvements in attitude, attention, discipline, behavior, test-taking and homework performance for all participants in the classroom. As a businessperson, when you experience difficulty with networking—for example, approaching someone at a gathering, asking for a referral, following up after meeting someone—it may almost feel as if you have a disability in that specific aspect of networking. The Brain Gym Balances, movements, and exercises in this book will allow you to immediately change your outcomes and improve your abilities and your successes.

The Elements of Brain Gym

The main methodology that Brain Gym uses is a process called the Balance. The Brain Gym process literally "balances" the brain and the body for specific tasks or goals by releasing past blockages or present difficulties and then re-educating the brain to allow for positive choices and actions. In this book I've created specific Balances, each of which is focused on an aspect of networking. For example, if you are having difficulty approaching people at networking events, you will do a Balance for that specific aspect. This Balance will switch you on to more easily and effectively approach people.

However, before you do a Balance, there are several other components that are used in the process that you need to know. They are:

- **Internal Biofeedback Responses:** You will learn to obtain responses from your mind-body connection using *one* of several different methods:
  1. Noticing

26

2. Self Muscle Checking
3. Muscle Checking with a Partner

Noticing and Self Muscle Checking are done by yourself, while a partner is necessary for Muscle Checking with a Partner. All of these biofeedback response methods will give you feedback to let you know when your body is switched-on by a stimuli and when it is switched off. You will also learn how to get "yes" and "no" responses from your body's own innate intelligence.

- **Brain Gym Movements and Exercises:** As discussed earlier, these movements and exercises are simple positions, exercises, or movements that re-wire the neural pathways in the brain for the goals you desire.

- **Calibration*:** This process is a series of steps, including Brain Gym movements and exercises that prepare a person for learning. Calibration is also done before beginning Noticing, Self Muscle Checking, or Muscle Checking with a Partner to confirm that the responses you are getting are accurate and that your mind and body are in a state of being ready to learn.

In the next chapter, we'll begin by discussing and explaining your Internal Biofeedback Responses.

---

* The protocol for Calibration is a variation of PACE, as it is taught in other Brain Gym classes.

CHAPTER 2
Internal Biofeedback Responses

Internal biofeedback responses are "answers" you receive from your own body. The goal is to collect data and information about the ways in which your mind and your body respond to specific stimuli. In other words, what switches you "off" and what switches you "on"? In order to do the Brain Gym processes, you'll first need to determine which method of biofeedback response works best for you. You'll learn this when you get to Chapter 3. But first let's look at the history of internal biofeedback response methods and why these methods work.

The History of Biofeedback Responses

The first system of biofeedback response that I learned, which I refer to as muscle checking, was developed by Dr. John Diamond in the late 1970s. Dr. Diamond was a psychiatrist who had become frustrated in his practice. During treatment, many of his patients would initially get better but, when they returned to the conditions that had caused or aggravated their problems in the first place, they would often backslide. Dr. Diamond searched for a way to identify their physical, nutritional, and emotional needs to help them achieve more long-lasting wellness. But despite all of his attempts, the conditions that caused his patients' psychological problems often eluded him. Dr. Diamond was on a mission to determine the specific triggers that caused or contributed to their illnesses so he could help eliminate them.

Dr. Diamond found an answer in a healing system called Applied Kinesiology and the decades-old system of muscle checking that it employs. Utilizing the muscle checking techniques, his research showed that the body is instantly switched off when it is impacted by negative emotional issues or mental stresses. He realized that muscle checking could be used to diagnose and treat emotional and mental health problems because it enabled him to isolate a patient's problems and therefore better understand its root causes. Once these specific stresses were identified, he was better able to assist his patients in finding ways to alter these stresses. Consequently, his patients got well faster and had fewer relapses.

Dr. Diamond then developed his own biofeedback response system, which he called Behavioral Kinesiology (BK), and found it to be an easy and accurate way to get information from the body's own innate intelligence. BK is used to "ask" the body what switches it on and what switches it off, as well as to obtain "yes" and "no" responses to questions.

Muscle checking allows you to determine exactly what forces, both external and internal, are stressful to your body. Then, once you identify the negative stresses in your life, you can focus on reducing, changing, or eliminating them. In this book you'll learn that the more stresses and negative programming that you eliminate from your life, the more energy and ability you will have available to accomplish what you want. You can read more about Dr. Diamond's breakthrough work in his books, *Your Body Doesn't Lie* (also published under the title *BK: Behavioral Kinesiology*) and *Life Energy* and in Jerry's book, *Switched-On Living.*

While this book focuses on your ability to network successfully, the bottom line is that every aspect of your life will benefit. Muscle checking can even be used to determine which elements of your environment switch you on and which elements switch you off. This includes the type of lighting used in your home or office, the color of your walls, and the music you listen to.

Dr. Diamond's muscle checking research has also demonstrated that there are many other factors that have either beneficial or adverse effects on the body's life energy. They include facial and bodily expressions, music, art, and graphics, and even modulations of the voice and emotions. He found that these reactions are almost universal—almost everyone has the same response to specific stimuli. These responses are not due to a person's beliefs, reasoning ability, or logic. For example, people are universally switched on when someone smiles at them, while a frown universally switches people off. Images of negative news events are weakening. These results are consistent no matter what background or culture the person being muscle checked comes from.

As I mentioned, Dr. Diamond developed Behavioral Kinesiology after studying the principles of Applied Kinesiology, which has been around for quite a while. Applied Kinesiology was developed in 1964 by a chiropractor, Dr. George Goodheart. It is a diagnostic and treatment system that incorporates muscle checking as an augment to medical examination and treatment procedures. It is used by doctors of chiropractic, osteopathy, homeopathy, dentistry, and medicine as well as by other trained professionals in the field of kinesiology.

Historically, however, muscle checking, which is also referred to as kinesiology, goes even further back in the medical annals. It was first discovered and developed as a system for diagnosis and treatment in 1912 by Dr. Robert Lovett of Harvard Medical School. Dr. Lovett, a professor of orthopedic surgery, first discovered the isolated muscle test in his work with paralyzed children. His goal was to measure the degree of muscle function in the partially or completely paralyzed little bodies of his patients. Referred to by Dr. Lovett as a "gravity test," a muscle associated with joint movement was positioned so that it was isolated and then tugged or pushed while the patient resisted. The degree to which the patient was able to resist determined the degree of integrity in the muscle. Thus, by isolating and testing muscles, a sensitive and individually specific means to determine muscle strength or weakness became available.

In the 1920s, Dr. Charles Lowman, an orthopedic surgeon, took this concept further. Then, in 1936, physical therapists Henry and Florence Kendall researched and wrote copiously about the use of the isolated muscle test for the purpose of determining muscle strength or weakness. In 1949, they published a book called *Muscles: Testing and Function.* Florence Kendall had impressive credentials; she was a consultant to the Surgeon General of the United States, a member of the Maryland State Board of Physical Therapy Examiners, a faculty member at the University of Maryland School of Medicine, and an instructor in Body Mechanics at Johns Hopkins Hospital.

Despite its proven efficacy, muscle checking was, to a great extent, "lost" with the beginning of World War II. By necessity, medical doctors moved into battlefield medicine, consisting mostly of surgery and drugs. Then, in 1964, Dr. George Goodheart rediscovered muscle checking and re-introduced it to the medical world through the diagnostic treatment modality he called Applied Kinesiology. Dr. John Thie then broke away from Applied Kinesiology and formed a group called Touch For Health that taught kinesiology to lay persons.

The next application came in 1981 with the work of Dr. Paul Dennison and Gail Dennison and their use of muscle checking as part of their Brain Gym processes. Dr. Dennison was working within Dr. Thie's organization when he started writing about his techniques.

Why Muscle Checking Works

Researchers believe that muscle checking works because of alterations in the functioning of the nervous system, leading to muscle strength or weakness. Muscle weakness can be attributed to various causes such as the blockage of an acupuncture meridian line, a chemical imbalance, or even a disturbing thought pattern.

Dr. David Hawkins, a psychiatrist, has been at the forefront of research on mental processes for decades. In the early 1970s, when the medical profession was resistant, even hostile, to the fact that nutrition has an impact on physical and mental health, Dr. Hawkins co-authored a book on that subject, *Orthomolecular Psychiatry*, with two-time Nobel Laureate Dr. Linus Pauling. Now a leading researcher on muscle checking, Dr. Hawkins explains the reasons it works in his book *Power Vs. Force*[10]:

> Each of us possesses a computer far more advanced than the most elaborate artificial intelligence machine available, one that's available at any time—the human mind itself. The basic function of any measuring device is simply to give a signal indicating the detection by the instrument of slight change … The reactions of the human body provide such a signal of change in conditions. As will be seen, the body can discern, to the finest degree, the

---

10 Hawkins, David, M.D., Ph.D., *Power Vs. Force: The Hidden Determinants of Human Behavior,* Hay House, Inc. 2002 (Revised Edition), page 44.

difference between that which is supportive of life and that which is not. This isn't surprising: After all, living things react positively to what is life-supportive and negatively to what is not; this is a fundamental mechanism of survival.

Another study that validates muscle checking as a diagnostic tool was done with 89 college students and published in *Perceptual and Motor Skills*[11]. The purpose of the study was to determine if a muscle is switched off when a person makes a false statement and if it remains switched on when the person makes a true statement. The study participants were asked to repeat four statements, two that were true and two that were false, and they were muscle checked after making each of the statements. They were asked to say, "My name is" and then state their real name. Then they were asked to say, "My name is" and say a name that was not theirs. They were also asked to say, "I am an American citizen" and "I am a Russian citizen." (All of the students selected for the study were American citizens.) The students were randomly assigned the order in which they were to make these statements. They did not know the purpose of the study, nor were any of them familiar with muscle checking.

The muscle checking was performed with sophisticated equipment that measured a combination of the pressure being applied by the person doing the muscle checking and the resistance of the muscle of the person being checked. The muscle checking was done by asking each participant to raise one arm out to their side and then resist while the other person pushed down on it. The researchers were looking at the variables of how long the person was able to keep the arm up and the amount of force that was necessary to push the arm down. The testing method differed from normal muscle checking in that the testers were pushing to the arm's fatigue level so that even on the strengthening statements the arm would eventually come down, but it took much more time and pressure to get it down. On false statements, they were

---

11 Muscle Test Comparisons of Congruent and Incongruent Self-Referential Statements by Daniel Monti, M.D., John Sinnott, Marc Marchese, Elisabeth J. S. Kunkel, Jeffrey M. Greeson, published in *Perceptual and Motor Skills,* 1999 (88, 1019-1028).

able to push the arm down an average of 58.9 percent faster and the amount of force used was an average of 17.2 percent less pressure than on the true statements. The results of this study showed scientifically significant validation that muscle checking is highly accurate.

Today, the effectiveness of muscle checking is clear to the myriad of people who use it on a regular basis. The applications and uses for muscle checking have proliferated over the years into many different methods that have been developed by researchers and health professionals. Here are some of the organizations and individuals who use or promote muscle checking:

- Dr. Goodheart established the International College of Applied Kinesiology, which publishes a research journal. Today many chiropractors use Applied Kinesiology in their practice. (See www.icak.com)
- Dr. John Thie's organization Touch for Health. (See www.tfhka.org)
- Neuro Emotional Technique (NET.), a method of chiropractic developed by Dr. Scott Walker, incorporates muscle checking to determine the emotional components of health problems. (See www.netmindbody.com)
- Nambudripad's Allergy Elimination Technique (NAET) was developed by Dr. Devi S. Nambudripad, a chiropractor and acupuncturist. As the name of this system implies, it is used to eliminate allergies. (See www.naet.com)
- Energy psychology healing systems, including Emotional Freedom Techniques (EFT), Thought Field Therapy (TFT), and Tapas Acupressure Technique (TAT) use muscle checking as an optional method of diagnosis in a process that clears emotional blocks. (See www.emofree.com; also see the Association for Comprehensive Energy Psychology at www.EnergyPsych.org for more on Energy Psychology)

Today there are many different applications for healing and well-being that employ kinesiology as a tool. The Energy Kinesiology Association has been formed to act as an umbrella organization to represent the field of kinesiology. (See www.EnergyK.org)

The Energy Impact of Visualization

Now I'd like you to do a simple exercise that will demonstrate how your mind can affect your body. Once you have that experience, we'll be reversing it so you can see how your body affects your mind. Visualization, the simple act of seeing something in your mind's eye, has many applications. It is one of many simple processes that can help you more easily reach the sales goals you want to achieve—and even take them to a new level of success.

Many studies confirm that "seeing" an activity in your mind's eye in as much detail as possible has a profound effect on the body's performance of that activity. Olympic and professional athletes have been trained to visualize every step of their routine or activity, all the way through to receiving the gold medal. One of the first to publicize the role of this body/mind connection in her success was Mary Lou Retton, a U.S. gymnast in the 1984 Olympics. Retton's coach taught her to do a visualization process each time she did her routine. She scored a ten on her last vault and won a gold medal. In total, she won five medals, the most won by any athlete at that Olympics.

Another example of the powerful positive effect of visualization comes from a research study of middle school kids. Three groups of seventh-grade boys and girls were asked to roll a ball at a target. The first group had thirteen hits on the first attempt. This group then practiced rolling the ball at the target for five minutes a day for seven days. When they were re-tested, they averaged a 70 percent improvement at hitting the target. The second group had twelve hits on their first attempt, almost as good as the first group. But then, instead of practicing with the ball, they were instructed to visualize rolling the ball and hitting the target. They practiced this visualization for five minutes a day for seven days. When they were retested using the actual ball, their improvement in hitting the target was 68 percent, almost as good as the group that had practiced with the ball.

The fascinating part of the study came with the third group. They also started out averaging twelve hits. Members of this group spent two-and-a-half minutes doing the visualization technique and then another two-and-a-half minutes actually rolling the ball every day for seven days. When they were retested in rolling the ball, this group had 31 hits, an improvement of 160 percent. The combination of visualization and physical action gave them a huge advantage over the groups that only physically practiced with the ball and the group that only did the visualization.[12]

To experience how powerful and fast visualizing is and how it can impact your body and your mind, do this simple exercise:

Arm Rotation Exercise

1. Stand up in a place where you can stretch your arms and rotate them without bumping into anything.

2. Keeping your feet firmly rooted in place, raise your right arm up in front of you like you are pointing to an object in the distance. Begin to rotate your arm slowly to the right until you reach your discomfort point. Hold it there for a second, noting how far your body has turned and where you are pointing towards with your fingers.

3. Rotate back to the front and put your arm down.

4. Now raise your right arm again and rotate to the right for a second time, noting how far your body has turned this time and where you are pointing with your fingers.

5. Rotate back to the front and put your arm down.

6. Close your eyes and, *without any movement of your body,* just visualize that you are raising your arm again and see your arm rotating to the right. This time see your arm rotating in a complete 360-degree circle with absolutely no pain or discomfort. Hold that thought for a few seconds. Then visualize that you are returning your arm back to the front position and then lowering it.

---

12 Cecelia A. Prediger, "Performance Enhancement Through Visualization," *Research Quarterly for Exercise and Sport,* Fall, 1988.

7. Now, with your eyes open, remembering to keep your feet firmly rooted in place, again raise your right arm up in front of you. Begin to rotate your arm slowly to the right until you reach your discomfort point. Hold it there for a second, noting how far your body has turned this time and where you are pointing towards with your fingers.

8. Rotate back to the front and put your arm down.

Were you surprised as to how much farther you could turn this third time? In my seminars, almost everyone is able to rotate farther after doing the visualization versus just doing the physical rotations the first two times. This is to demonstrate to you the power of your mind on your body. This applies to you in your networking, enabling you to visualize and focus on the goals, directions, and results you want to achieve. In the next chapter, we will show you how Brain Gym allows you to experience the reverse of the mind affecting the body by seeing your body's power to affect your mind.

CHAPTER 3

CHOOSING YOUR PREFERRED METHOD OF BIOFEEDBACK RESPONSE

In the Brain Gym process you have the option of using one of three different methods of internal biofeedback response. Follow these instructions and you will discover for yourself the amazing ability your body has to simply and easily tell you what it finds positive and beneficial and what it finds negative and difficult in the selling process.

The three Methods of Internal Biofeedback Response are:
1. Muscle Checking with a Partner
2. Self Muscle Checking
3. Noticing

Let's look at them one by one.

Muscle Checking with a Partner

With this method you'll need to find a partner so you can "muscle check" each other. If you don't have a partner handy, read on anyway—and be sure to do the muscle checking on a partner at a later time. Also, you can see a demonstration of muscle checking in a free online video at www.SwitchedOnNetworking.com/demo.

Muscle Checking with a Partner involves your partner applying physical pressure to your arm muscle. As you'll see, you don't have to be physically strong to do the check or to be checked. The key concept in the checking is that everything around us and within us can affect our muscle strength. Basically, when you apply a steady pressure on your partner's extended arm, her arm will stay up and remain switched-on when she is exposed to a positive thought or a situation that she views positively. Her arm muscle will be switched-off and come down when she is exposed to a negative thought or a situation that she views negatively. This will make more sense to you as you proceed.

In some cases, the results of muscle checking can be influenced by the people involved or by the environment. In order to avoid impacting the results, both the person doing the muscle check and the person being checked should avoid facial expressions, especially smiles and frowns, and there should be no music playing.

There are two ways to do Muscle Checking with a Partner—one method uses a hard pressure and the other uses a lighter pressure. First we'll look at the way to do it using the hard pressure.

Muscle Checking with a Partner Using Hard Pressure
Step I. Finding Normal Response

Before doing a muscle check for any specific stimuli, you need to check the person in neutral to find their normal response level.

1. Face your partner. Ask if he has any pains or discomforts with either arm or shoulder. If not, continue this process. If your partner has an issue, then use the arm and shoulder that does not have any pain or discomfort. If both are in pain or discomfort, then do not do this process.

2. Ask your partner to raise one arm up from the side of the body so it is at a right angle to the body and level with the shoulder, with the thumb pointing toward the floor. Imagine a bird with a wing outstretched and you'll have the correct arm position. The other arm remains at the side of the body.

3. Now place one of your hands on your partner's extended arm, just above the wrist. Place your other hand on your partner's opposite shoulder.

4. Instruct your partner to resist as you push down, firmly and steadily, with a hard pressure, on the extended arm. As you are about to push down on your partner's arm, say out loud to your partner "Ready—resist." You are not attempting to force her arm down; her arm should stay fairly level while you are applying

the pressure. You do want it to be a hard, steady pressure on the arm in order to measure her normal level of resistance. You should press firmly for several seconds and then release.

If her arm goes down more than an inch or two during this check for her normal response level, you are using too much force. If that occurred, then do it again, remembering that the amount of pressure applied should be based on the person's level of strength. As an example, you would press harder when you are muscle checking a football player and more gently if you are muscle checking a petite person.

When you apply the pressure on the extended arm, you are checking a muscle called the lateral deltoid. As you'll experience in Step II, when a negative stimulus occurs, your partner's arm will go down easily when you apply the same amount of pressure. This will signify through the deltoid muscle that the entire body's energy level is in a switched-off state. When the arm stays up, it will indicate that the person's energy is switched-on. You can use other muscles in your body to do muscle checking, such as the leg muscles; however, the deltoid muscle is easy and conveniently located for this purpose.

Step II.   Muscle Checking a Stimulus

Now that you've found the person's normal response level, you are ready to do a muscle checking procedure for a specific stimulus. If, during the muscle checking, the person's arm that is being checked becomes tired, you can simply have the person switch to the other arm. Just be sure to check the "new" arm first for its normal level of resistance before you do any further checking.

We'll start out with a muscle checking procedure that shows how your partner's thoughts impact her body's energy by having her think about a negative networking experience she has had.

1. Check your partner for Normal response as we did in Step I above.

2. While your partner keeps her arm extended, ask her to close her eyes and think of a very negative networking

experience. Ask her to nod her head when she has this thought firmly pictured or felt in her mind. Then tell her to resist while you press down. Her arm will go down easily even if she is resisting with all her might. This means thinking this negative thought has switched her off.

3. Now tell your partner to resume the arm-extended position while thinking of a very positive networking experience. Again, ask her to close her eyes and nod her head when she is focused on this image. Then tell her to resist as you push down. Her arm will stay level and it may feel even stronger than when you first checked her for Normal response. She is now demonstrating a switched-on response to the muscle checking.

4. Switch roles and have your partner check you.

You will probably notice that when your partner thinks about a very negative experience, it takes very little pressure to push the arm down. Conversely, when the person thinks about a very positive experience, the arm stays switched-on even if you use more pressure when attempting to push it down.

Muscle Checking with a Partner Using Light Pressure

Now that you know how to muscle check using strong pressure, you can experience this alternative method which uses much less pressure. The same muscle will respond with one-fifth of the pressure used in the "hard pressure" muscle checking. This is helpful because a person's arm tends to tire after a few rounds of hard pressure checking. With the lighter pressure, this fatigue is avoided.

Another difference in the Light Pressure Muscle Checking method is that the person who is being checked is the one who determines when he is ready for the pressure to be applied by saying "push." Because there is a tendency for a person to hold his breath when the person doing the checking presses, possibly affecting the results, the word "push" is stretched out to become "Pusssssshhhhhhh." This keeps the person breathing. Here's how to do Light Pressure Muscle Checking:

Light Pressure Muscle Checking for Normal Response
1. Face your partner.
2. Ask your partner to raise one arm up from the side of the body so it is at a right angle to the body and level with the shoulder, with the thumb pointing toward the floor. This is the same position as in hard muscle checking.
3. Place just two or three fingers of your hand just above her wrist. Put your other hand on her opposite shoulder.
4. Ask your partner being checked to say "Pusssshhhhh" when she is ready to resist and then lightly push down on her arm for a couple of seconds, using just a fraction

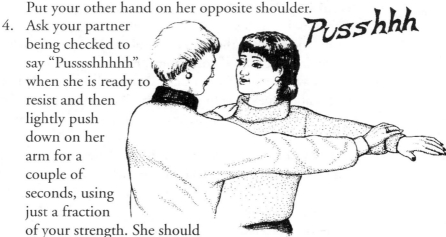

of your strength. She should be able to easily keep her arm up. If you also look at her shoulder, there should have been no movement taking place. If there was, it means you need to press more lightly. In that case repeat this light pressure again so that there is no movement in the shoulder. This will give you the correct "reading" of the amount of pressure to use with Light Pressure Checking.

When you do the Switched-On Networking Balances in the upcoming chapters you will have the option of using either Light or Hard Pressure Muscle Checking. Keep in mind that both of these types of Muscle Checking require a partner. If you don't have a partner available, you'll need to use a Self Muscle Checking or a Noticing method as your biofeedback response mechanism instead. They are explained in the next section.

There are several things to watch for to make sure the Light Pressure Checking gives you an accurate response. Let's look at the example of the muscle checking we did earlier in this chapter for a negative networking experience. As you'll recall, when the person who was being muscle checked *thought* about a negative networking experience, this thought caused her body to switch off and her arm went down. Though it is rare, let's imagine that you got inappropriate results from this muscle checking—meaning that your partner's arm stayed up when she thought of the negative experience. There are several reasons you might be getting an inappropriate response. They include:

- **Recruiting Other Muscles:** Your partner could be *recruiting* other muscles to help prevent her arm from going down. To do this, she may tilt the whole side of the body up or just raise the shoulder area up. If you observe recruiting, tell her to make sure to have the thumb pointing downward and to only tighten the shoulder muscle as this more specifically isolates the lateral deltoid muscle which is the muscle you are using to measure your response.
- **Faders:** Your partner could be a *fader*. When you press down with this lighter pressure, she may initially appear switched-on with the arm staying up. However, if you continue to hold the pressure for a couple of seconds, her ability to keep her arm up will begin to fade and her arm will go down. Therefore, it's important to press on a person's arm for several seconds so you don't miss the person who is a fader.

Looking for a Mushy Arm Response: The arm may only go down a little bit as you are checking your partner while she is thinking the negative thought. That's okay. I describe this as the arm going "mushy." With the lighter pressure you are only looking for subtle differences between the arm staying switched-on and becoming switched-off. (If you are unsure of what "mushy" is, you can do the Hard Pressure Muscle Checking described on page 40 as you will get a clearer reading of what is switched-off; however, keep in mind your partner's arm might tire faster. Before doing the hard pressure, warn him that you are switching to using this level of pressure.)

Light Pressure Muscle Checking for "Yes"/"No" Responses

Light Pressure Muscle Checking is also used to get "yes" or "no" answers to questions. To determine how this works, follow these instructions:

1. Follow Steps 1 through 4 of Light Pressure Muscle Checking for Normal response.

2. Say out loud to your partner who is being muscle checked: "Your body will demonstrate a 'yes' response." Then ask your partner to say "Pussssshhhhh" as you muscle check his arm with the light pressure. His arm will stay up.

3. Say out loud to your partner: "Your body will demonstrate a 'no' response." Then ask your partner to say "Pussssshhhhh" as you muscle check his arm; his arm will go down. (Remember to be aware of recruiters and faders as discussed above.)

As amazing as it may seem, through the use of muscle checking your body is capable of answering specific questions. The person being checked or the person doing the checking can ask questions framed in a "yes" or "no" format. This ability to obtain answers to "yes" and "no" questions allows you to access and understand how all parts of the networking process are affecting your networking abilities both consciously and subconsciously.

Self Muscle Checking Methods

The pioneers in this field, such as Dr. John Thie and Bruce Dew found that it is also possible to get biofeedback responses from the body by muscle checking yourself. Self Muscle Checking is the second method of physical biofeedback response that I use when I am teaching the Switched-On seminars.

There are six different self-muscle checking methods presented here to get "yes/switched-on" or "no/switched-off responses" from your body. Most people find that one or more of these six methods work well for them; although every now and then I encounter a person for whom none of them work. So you'll need to experiment with each of them to see if any work for you and, if several do, decide which one you prefer to use. (If you're one of those for whom none of the Self Muscle Checking methods work, you will need to do Muscle Checking with a Partner or one of the Noticing methods which is presented in the next section.)

As a reminder, you can see these methods demonstrated in a free online video at www.SwitchedOnNetworking.com/demo.

Self Muscle Checking Method 1: Links in a Chain

1. Place the tip of your thumb and the tip of your index finger of one hand together as though you are making an "okay" sign or a circle. Hold them together firmly.
2. Link together the index finger and thumb of the other hand inside the circle made by the first hand. It's as if you are forming two links in a chain. You will first be determining a Normal response level by attempting to pull your two circles apart. Use a steady, strong pressure but don't pull so hard that you pull the circles apart. Ask your body (silently or out loud) to give you a "yes/switched-on" response as you attempt to pull your links apart. You should be unable to pull your fingers apart with this level of force.

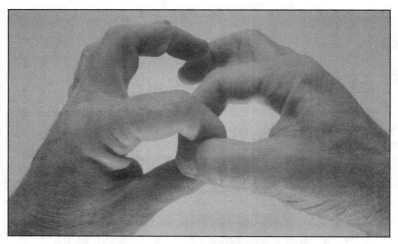

3. Ask your body (silently or out loud) to demonstrate a "no/switched-off" response and again attempt to pull your links apart. This time, the links should be easily broken and you should be able to pull your fingers through.
4. If you don't notice a difference, then you'll need to see if the next method works for you.

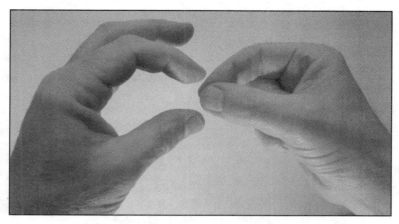

Self Muscle Checking Method 2: Threading the Needle

1. Once again place the tip of your thumb and the tip of your index finger of one hand together as though you are making an "okay" sign or a circle. Hold them together firmly.

2. With the other hand put the pads of your index finger and thumb together. Now, insert these two fingers into the circle formed by the two fingers in Step 1. It's as if you're threading the eye of a needle with your second hand. Expand these two inner fingers so you are pushing against the fingers in the outer circle. Don't push so hard that the outside circle fingers break contact.

3. Ask your body (silently or out loud) to give you a "yes/switched on" response and attempt to open the two inner fingers. The outside circle fingers should remain in contact.

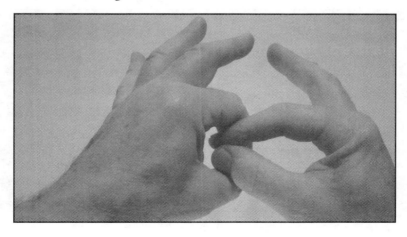

4. Ask your body (silently or out loud) to demonstrate a "no switched-off" response and attempt to open the two inner fingers. This time, the outer circle formed by the thumb and index finger should separate when you push against it with the fingers that are on the inside.

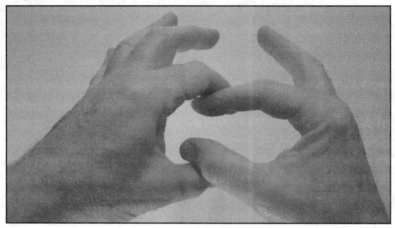

If you don't notice a difference, go to the next method.

Self Muscle Checking Method 3: Index and Middle Finger

Using one hand, place the pad of the middle finger on top of the index finger nail. With the middle finger, push down on the index finger. Say the "yes/switched-on" statement and the index finger will stay straight.

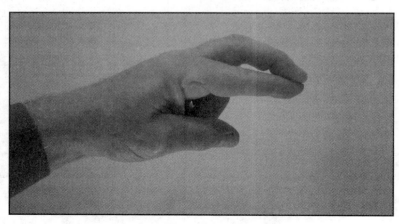

Say the "no/switched-off" statement and the index finger will bend downward. If you don't notice a difference, go to the next method.

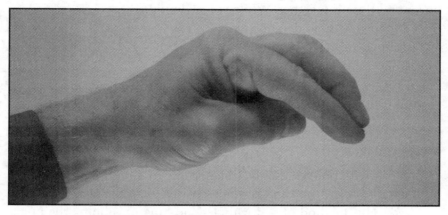

Self Muscle Checking Method 4: Thigh Muscle

While sitting in a chair, raise one foot a few inches off the floor. Place your hand on the thigh muscle. Say the "yes/switched-on" statement and push down on your thigh muscle. It will stay up. Say the "no/switched-off" statement and the leg will go down. If you don't notice a difference, go to the next method.

"Yes/Switched-on response."   "No/Switched-off response."

Self Muscle Checking Method 5: Skin Response

On each hand lightly and quickly rub your index finger and thumb together. While you're doing that, ask your body to demonstrate a "yes/switched-on" response. The fingers should continue to move easily. Next, ask for a "no/switched-off" response while continuing to rub the fingers together. It will become sticky and harder to move the fingers. If you don't notice a difference, go to the next method. (While you can do this with one hand only, I like people to do it initially with both hands in case one hand is more sensitive than the other.)

Note: This method of Self Muscle Checking of rubbing the finger and thumb together is based on the same principle as a lie detector test in which the electrical resistance of the skin, called the galvanic skin response, is measured. The galvanic skin response registers immediate changes in the skin's conductivity, which varies when the nervous system triggers changes in the body's internal state.

Self Muscle Checking Method 6: Body Rocking

In this method, the body "rocks" or tilts slightly forward for a "yes/switched-on" response and slightly backward for a "no/switched-off" response.

1. To get a "yes/switched-on" response:
   Stand with your eyes closed. Say silently to yourself that your body will identify a "yes/switched on" response. You should feel your body tilting forward slightly. This forward tilt will be your "yes/switched-on" response.
2. To get a "no/ switched-off" response:
   Stand with your eyes closed. Say silently to yourself that your body will identify a "no/switched-off" response. You should experience your body tilting backward slightly. This backward tilt will be identified as a "no/switched-off" response.

Once you have determined this baseline for the body rock, you can use this as your method of self muscle checking. You can also do it with your eyes open.

As I said earlier, one of these Self Muscle Checking methods works for most people. If that's not the case for you, you'll have the option to explore the two alternate ways to do Noticing that is introduced below.

Noticing

Noticing relies on you to notice what is going on inside your body as your *inner guide*. With Noticing, you'll need to pay special attention to your feelings, posture, body sensations, and breathing. Noticing is an easy method of biofeedback response because it simply involves becoming attuned to your body's constant internal communications system. With this method you stop what you are doing and *notice* the feelings and sensations that may be causing you to be switched-on or switched-off. There are two methods of Noticing. You can use whichever one you are more comfortable with. Let's begin with the first Noticing method.

First Noticing Method—Observing Your Body's Responses
In this first Noticing technique you will observe what's going on in your body. To do this technique you'll need to stand up and put your hands at the sides of your body. Read the instructions below and then follow them without adjusting your body's position. You are just observing your body's responses.

1. Close your eyes and think of a negative networking situation, such as feeling uncomfortable when asking for a referral, or awkwardness when you attempted to connect with someone at an event. Really focus on your negative thoughts about it.
2. Keeping your eyes closed and without adjusting your body, observe your physical posture for a few seconds.
3. Next, observe your breathing for a few seconds.
4. Observe if you are you experiencing discomfort or pain in an parts of your body.
5. Finally, observe what's going on in your mind. What kind of thoughts are you having? Is your mind churning?

What did you observe? While there is no one right answer, most people report that they observed at least one of the following: that their physical posture was slumped, their breathing was shallow, they had pain somewhere on their body and their mind was churning. I call these responses a switched-off response. If your observations were different, that's okay. Remember, Noticing is not judging, it's just paying attention to what's going on in your body.

Now let's have you do the same thing again, except this time you are going to be focusing on a very positive networking situation. Again, you are just observing your body's responses you are not adjusting it.

1. Close your eyes and think of a positive networking situation. Really focus on your positive thoughts about it.
2. Without adjusting your body, first observe your physical posture for a few seconds.
3. Next, observe your breathing for a few seconds.
4. Observe if you are still experiencing discomfort or pain in any parts of your body?
5. Finally, observe what's going on in your mind, in particular, any thoughts that you are having.

So what did you observe? When thinking of a positive networking situation most people report that they observed a change in the areas that they noticed the first time: that their physical posture was upright, their breathing was deeper, they had no pain in their body and that their mind was calmer. I call these responses a switched-on response. If your observations were different, that's okay. Again, Noticing is not judging, it's just paying attention to what's going on in your body and your mind, but it is great feedback that enables us to observe the ways our thoughts immediately affect our mind-body system.

The positive response you had in your body and mind will be used as your definition of a yes/switched-on response as you go through the book. The negative response you had will be used as a no/switched-off response.

Second Noticing Method—Using Reference Points

To use this method, you will have to first establish specific locations on your body to what it means to have a "switched-on" or "switched-off" response. The visualization technique that follows will help you establish this baseline. You can also apply your responses to getting a "yes" or a "no" response.

<u>*To locate a "switched-on" response in your body:*</u>

Sit quietly with your eyes closed and visualize or remember a past networking experience that you feel was positive and fulfilling. As you begin to recall this experience in your mind, take a few seconds to intensify the thought. Once this feeling is intensified, locate it at a specific place on your body. Take ten to fifteen seconds to intensify the feelings at this location on your body. Say silently to yourself that this location will be identified as a "switched-on" response. Some examples of these internal feelings and awareness can include:

- A feeling of ease or automatic movement
- A feeling of joy
- A physical sensation somewhere in or on your body
- A subtle movement
- A smile coming across your face
- A specific movement of eye, head, etc.
- A feeling of calm

<u>*To locate a "switched-off" response in your body:*</u>

Continue sitting quietly with your eyes closed and visualize or remember a past experience that was difficult or negative. As you begin to recall this experience in your mind, take a few seconds to intensify the thought. Once this feeling is intensified, locate it at a place on your body. Take ten to fifteen seconds to intensify the feeling at that location on your body. Say silently to yourself that this location will be identified as a "switched-off" response. Some examples of these internal feelings and awareness can include:

- A feeling of doubt
- A feeling of disappointment
- A physical sensation somewhere in your body

- A frown coming across your face
- A specific movement of your eye, head, etc.
- A feeling of tension
- Uncertainty in a new situation

Once you have determined this baseline for the internal experience of "switched-on" reactions and the comparable "switched-off" reactions of the body, you can use this as your method of Noticing.

Using Noticing in the Balance Process
You can use either of the Noticing techniques as you go through the balance process at the end of each of Donna's upcoming chapters. Just notice if your body is feeling the way it did when you were thinking the positive thought in the first Noticing method. If you are using the second Noticing method then you will get a response at a place on your body where you identified either the "yes/switched-on" response or the "no/switched-off" one.

Which Internal Biofeedback Response Method Should You Use?
As you are going through the balance steps in the coming sections of this book, you will choose which method you will be using: Muscle Checking with a Partner, Self Muscle Checking or Noticing. Even if you are doing one of the physical checking methods, I suggest that you also start Noticing internally whether you are switched-on or switched-off so you are also becoming comfortable with that method.

You can also switch methods each time you do a Balance. I find that each individual will gravitate to one or two methods that they are most comfortable with. Just start out with one of them and go from there.

The Energy Impact of Your Thoughts and Attitudes
All of the biofeedback response methods will glean the same results. They prove that negative thoughts and experiences, such as rejection in a networking situation, are draining to your body's energy. And simply thinking about a positive networking experience is strengthening.

However, while your energy is raised by thinking of a positive thought, *it is switched-on only as long as you maintain that thought.* If you return to viewing the situation negatively again, the draining impact will return.

Changing Your Mind

The instructions below use Muscle Checking with a Partner to demonstrate this, although you can use Self Muscle Checking or Noticing if you prefer. Just adapt the instructions as needed.

1. Check your partner for Normal response.
2. Ask your partner to close her eyes and visualize a negative networking experience in her mind. Muscle check her with either the Hard or Light Pressure method. Her arm will go down, meaning she's switched-off.
3. Next, ask her to switch the negative experience and find something about it to view positively even if it's just being glad the situation is over.
4. Ask her to shake her head to indicate that she has made the switch.
5. Tell her to resist and press down on her arm. Her arm will remain switched-on.
6. Have her repeat the negative thought again and check her. Her arm will go down again.
7. Have her repeat switching to the positive thought again and check her. Her arm will remain switched-on this time.

This exercise shows us once again the incredible power of the mind. By *changing your mind* about how you view a situation, you can temporarily alter the impact the experience is having on you. All you need to do is to *decide* to think positively about the experience. While this is easy to say, I grant you that it can be difficult to maintain positive thoughts about a situation that is challenging to you. That's why I say it is temporary. And that's where the Brain Gym Balances, which you'll learn to do in Chapter 6, come into play. These Balances are life changing because they re-educate your mind-body system to eliminate your negative thoughts about the stressful aspects of the networking process. For example, in the Balance for a Positive Networking Attitude, you'll learn two Brain Gym techniques that will allow you to completely eliminate the negative charge from the negative networking situation you just pictured in only two minutes. This means after you've completed that Balance, you'll be able to think of the same situation but it will no longer have a negative impact on you.

CHAPTER 4

BRAIN GYM MOVEMENTS AND EXERCISES

There are four main components to a Brain Gym Balance:
1. Biofeedback responses from the body using one of three methods you just learned in Chapter 3: Muscle Checking with a Partner, Self Muscle Checking or Noticing
2. Brain Gym movements and exercises, which are covered in this chapter.
3. Calibration (which you'll learn in the next chapter)
4. The Balance itself, which you'll learn in Chapter 6.

Using Brain Gym Movements to Re-Wire and Rebalance the Brain

Brain Gym movements are specific exercises that correlate to the way in which we perform different tasks, motor skills, and activities. In his book, *Brain Gym and Me,* Paul Dennison, Ph.D., the creator of Brain Gym, explains it this way: "The Brain Gym movements have been designed to activate various cognitive functions, including communication, organization, and comprehension. The movements are effective because they activate the brain in specific ways that ready us for learning. Brain Gym strengthens the physical skills involved in the learning process, and when we feel physically prepared to meet the day, the mental aspect of our learning comes more easily." [13]

When used in conjunction with Balances (which you'll learn in the next chapter), these movements re-wire and rebalance the neural pathways in your brain. As I previously discussed, when you have an aspect of

---

13 Dennison, Paul D., Ph.D., *Brain Gym and Me*, Edu-Kinesthetics, Inc., 2006, page 46.

networking you don't like to do, it's harder for you to be successful with it. In minutes, the Brain Gym movements balance and integrate your brain's hemispheres quickly and easily so what was difficult becomes easy. Some of the Brain Gym exercises require physical movement, which you should do slowly, while others are easy positions which you simply hold for thirty to sixty seconds.

These Brain Gym movements and exercises are very easy to do and can have an extremely positive impact on your business success. In networking, this will be especially true when you plug Donna's networking strategies into your efforts. (Donna's strategies begin in Chapter 6 and then are continued in Part II, starting on page 101.)

The History of Brain Gym Movements

Many of the Brain Gym movements in this book were originally developed more than seventy years ago in the fields of behavioral optometry and sensorimotor training, while others were adapted from acupressure and yoga. Over the years, a number of leading pioneers in the learning and health fields created their own variations on these movements.

In the early 1970s, Dr. John Thie created Touch for Health, a system for natural health that included brain integration techniques as well as other methods such as acupressure, touch, and massage to improve postural balance and reduce physical and mental pain and tension. Dr. Thie's book, *Touch for Health* was published in 1973.

In addition to the work of Dr. Paul Dennison and Gail Dennison, who created Brain Gym, a number of other pioneers have used or adapted Brain Gym movements in their work. They include: Gordon Stokes and Daniel Whiteside *(One Brain: Dyslexic Learning Correction and Brain Integration)*, Dr. Carla Hannaford *(Smart Moves: Why Learning is Not All in Your Head)*, Dr. Charles Krebs *(A Revolutionary Way of Thinking)*, Sharon Promislow *(Making the Brain/Body Connection)*, Laurie Glazener *(Sensorcises: Active Enrichment for the Out-of-Step Learner)* and Cecilia Koester *(Movement Based Learning for Children of All Abilities)*. Educators and trainers who use Brain Gym movements in their classes include Paul Scheele of Learning Strategies Corporation and T. Harv Eker of Peak Potential Training.

Brain Gym Movements and Exercises

I'd like you to do the Brain Gym movements and exercises in this section so you will understand how simple and easy they are to perform. As you continue with this book, you will be told which Brain Gym movements to use as you do each of the Balances. It is the Brain Gym movements and exercises that actually re-wire and rebalance the brain.

In addition to learning how to do each of the Brain Gym movements below, you will also find an explanation of what that specific movement does in the brain and the body. It's important that you do Brain Gym movements slowly to allow the brain and body to make more neural connections.

Alphabet 8s

Figure 1

Center a piece of paper in front of you. With a pen or pencil, begin by drawing continuous and overlapping infinity symbols or the number 8 which is lying on its side. (Figure 1)

Step 1: Draw three infinity symbols using your left hand, then three using your right hand, then three using both hands together. Your eyes remain focused on the point of your pen or pencil. (Figure 1)

Step 2: *The letter a:* Draw three infinity symbols with your normal writing hand. Without stopping, draw a lower case letter "a" on top of the left-hand side of the 8. Without stopping, do two more infinity symbols. (Figure 2)

Figure 2

Step 3: *The letter b:* Draw three more infinity symbols. Without stopping, draw a lower case letter "b" on the right-hand side of the infinity symbol. Again without stopping, do two more infinity symbols. (Figure 2)

Step 4: *The letter c & d:* Repeat the same sequence, drawing a letter "c" on the left side of the infinity symbol, and then repeat the same sequence drawing a "d" on the left side. (Figure 3)

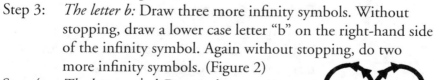

Figure 3

59

You only need to draw these four letters.

Explanation: Alphabet 8s integrates the left and right visual fields while also increasing left and right hemispheric integration. This may enhance creative writing, spelling, and peripheral vision. Reading, writing, and concentration skills improve.

Arm Activation

Lift your right arm straight up toward the ceiling keeping it as close to your ear as you can. Place your left hand on the front of the right arm muscle. As you slowly and gently exhale through your mouth, do an isometric movement by pushing your right arm against your left hand without letting your right arm move. Continue pressing for about seven seconds. Inhale as you relax your pressure. Place your left hand on the back of your arm and press again for seven seconds. Repeat this procedure, pressing against the outside of your right arm and then against the inside of your right arm. Each time exhale for seven seconds.

Repeat the entire sequence for the other arm.

Explanation: Arm Activation lengthens the muscles of the upper chest and shoulders, where muscular control for both gross and fine motor activities originates. This movement improves focus and concentration, enhances one's ability to express ideas, and helps one have a longer attention span for doing paperwork.

Balance Buttons

Place three or more fingertips about two inches behind your left ear, about three finger widths away from the ear. Place your other hand on your belly button. Move just your eyes slowly back and forth. Looking first to the far left then move your eyes to the far right. Continue to move your eyes back and forth without straining. Do this for thirty seconds.

Change hands and repeat on the other side for 30 seconds.

Explanation: Balance Buttons appears to stimulate the body's balance system through the inner ear. This restores your sense of equilibrium, relaxing your eyes and the rest of your body and freeing your attention for easier thought and action. This improves one's ability to make decisions, concentrate and problem solve.

Belly Breathing

Place your hands on your stomach. Begin by inhaling through the mouth into the stomach. Your hands should move outward with the inhalation. Begin to exhale through your mouth, in short little puffs of air as if you are keeping a feather floating in the air. Continue to exhale until your lungs feel empty. Again inhale deeply, filling your stomach. This time don't exhale in short puffs; instead do a slow and complete exhalation.

Repeat this deep inhalation and exhalation for three or four breaths.

Explanation: Belly Breathing improves oxygen consumption and blood circulation to the brain and the central nervous system while increasing one's energy level. It improves diaphragmatic breathing which has been found to improve both reading and speaking abilities.

Brain Buttons

Place one hand on your belly button. With the thumb and middle finger of the other hand, locate the two hollow areas below the collarbone. The hollows are one or two inches away from the sternum which is the bone that runs down the center of the chest.

Rub these areas vigorously for thirty seconds.

Explanation: Brain Buttons improves digital and hand-eye coordination for writing and computer work while relaxing neck and shoulder muscles. It also improves body balance and enhances energy levels.

61

Double Doodle

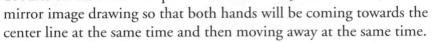

Take a piece of paper. You are going to draw mirror images on the paper using both hands simultaneously. Begin by drawing a line down the center of the paper. Next, draw identical doodles on each side. Keep in mind this is mirror image drawing so that both hands will be coming towards the center line at the same time and then moving away at the same time.

Continue for thirty seconds.

Explanation: Double Doodle drawing using both hands establishes directionality and orientation in space relative the center line running down the front of the body. This assists in developing hand-eye coordination for improved writing skills, spelling, and math. It also improves ones ability to skim and scan what is being read.

Earth Buttons

Place two fingers from one hand under the lower lip. Put the heel of the other hand on the navel with the fingers pointing downward. Wherever your fingers reach, rest them on the body. With just your eyes moving and not your head, look at the floor for a couple of second and gradually raise your eyes to the ceiling as if you are tracing your eyes up a straight column and then immediately look down again. Keep moving your eyes from down to up.

Repeat this ten times. Continue to breathe.

Explanation: Earth Buttons are located on the center line running down the front of the body. Holding these points stimulates the brain and relieves mental fatigue, as well as increases organizational skills and enhances the ability to focus on close objects such as computer screens.

Hook-Ups

This movement is done in two parts. It can be done seated or standing:

Part I ...

Clasp your hands together. Whichever thumb is on top will be considered your primary side. Release your hands and extend your hands in front of you with the back of each hand facing the other. Cross the primary side hand over the top of the other hand and intertwine your fingers. Bring your clasped hands under and into your chest. Cross your primary side ankle in front of the other ankle. Place your tongue against the roof of your mouth, one quarter inch behind your front teeth. Keep breathing through your nose. The first time you do this keep your eyes closed. Hold for thirty seconds to one minute.

Part II ...

Uncross your legs and release your hands. Place the fingertips of both of your hands together forming a teepee. Keep your eyes closed the first time you do this, the tongue up, and continue to breathe. Hold for thirty seconds to one minute.

Explanation: Hook-ups is a variation of an exercise originally developed by Wayne Cook, an expert on electromagnetic energy. Part I connects all the energy circuits in the body at the same time and stimulates the movement of any blocked energy. Touching fingertips in Part II balances and connects the two hemispheres of the brain. This reduces stress while raising comfort levels in new situations, enhances balance and coordination, and improves one's ability to listen and speak.

Lazy 8s

Place your left arm extended straight out in front of you with the thumb pointing towards the ceiling. Focus your eyes on that thumb.

Without taking your eyes off your thumb, keep your head facing straight forward, while you trace a large infinity sign or the number 8 lying on its side in the air slowly and smoothly.

Begin to trace your Lazy 8 at the center point of the 8 and go up and to the left side with your hand. Do three full Lazy 8s with one hand, then do three with the other, and, finally, do three of them with both hands clasped together. Remember to keep your head facing forward.

Explanation: Lazy 8s integrate the left and right visual fields while also increasing left and right hemispheric integration which improves balance and coordination. Many people report better binocular vision and increased peripheral vision after doing the Lazy 8s. Reading, writing, and comprehension skills improve as these tasks become easier.

Space Buttons

Place two fingers above the lip. Place your other hand on your tailbone. While keeping your nose facing straight ahead, look up with your eyes toward the ceiling for a few seconds. Imagine a column in front of you running from the ceiling to the floor. Gradually lower your eyes down the column to the floor. Immediately raise them up to the ceiling and hold them for a couple of seconds in that position. Repeat this up and down movement ten times while you continue to breathe.

Explanation: Space Buttons are located at the top and bottom of the central nervous system which includes: the spinal column, back brain, midbrain (which is the portion of the brain located behind the eyes and nose) and cerebral cortex. Holding the two points stimulates movement throughout the system, which improves attention, focus, motivation, and intuition for decision-making.

The Calf Pump

This movement is similar to a runner's stretch.

Place your hands shoulder-width apart against a wall, leaning your body at a 45-degree angle to the wall. Place your right foot in front of the body with the knee bent and extend the left leg out straight behind you, keeping the leg straight.

Imagine you have a string coming out the top of your head. As you exhale, raise your left heel off the floor, while keeping your left leg straight. As you inhale, lower the left heel to the floor.

Do this a total of three times then switch leg positions and repeat three times. The more you bend the knee in the front, the more stretch you will feel in the calf muscle.

Explanation: The Calf Pump restores a more natural length to the muscles and tendons in the back of the body. This improves attention and focus while creating a deeper feeling of relaxation. It also improves written and spoken communications while increasing the ability to plan, complete projects, and anticipate finishing the project.

The Cross Crawl

Slowly march in place like a drum majorette. As your right arm swings up, your left leg moves up, allowing you to touch the right hand to the left knee (or as close as you can get). Next, swing the left arm and the right leg up so that you touch the left hand to the right knee. When you make this movement, you are automatically crossing the midline of your body. (The midline runs down the center of the body. If you draw a straight line from your nose down past the belly button, that's where the midline is located).

Continue to do The Cross Crawl movement slowly for thirty to sixty seconds.

Variations of The Cross Crawl:

There are other ways to achieve the effect of The Cross Crawl. You might want to experience each of them.

- Instead of touching your hand to the opposite leg, reach your hand down and touch the opposite heel. Continue by alternating touching opposite hand to the opposite heel.
- Use your elbows instead of your hand to touch the knee. Continue by alternating touching the opposite elbow to the opposite knee. This variation of The Cross Crawl stretches the core stomach muscles and gives the body even more stretch.
- Move your left heel behind you and touch your heel with your right hand. Continue by alternating touching opposite hands and heels behind the body.

Explanation: When you use one hand to touch the knee on the opposite side of your body, you are crossing the midline of your body. This activates both sides of your brain and body simultaneously. It is called a heterolateral movement because both the left and right hemispheres of the brain have to cooperate for your left hand and your right knee to be at the correct place at the same time so that contact can occur. Because The Cross Crawl activates both brain hemispheres simultaneously, it engages the brain for coordinating visual, auditory, and kinesthetic abilities. This exercise improves such skills as listening, reading, writing and memory—all valuable tools for networking.

The Elephant

Stand with your feet about shoulder-width apart. Bend your knees. Point your right arm straight down to the floor in front of you. Lean your head so that the right ear touches or is close to your right shoulder. Point your finger and begin to trace a large infinity sign or number 8 lying on its side, in the air with your extended arm. Focus your eyes slightly past your fingertips. Keep breathing as you move. Start by going up the center and to your left side. As you do the upper loop of the 8, straighten your legs. As you do the lower loop, bend your legs again.

Do this a total of three times, then repeat with the left arm.

Explanation: The Elephant releases muscle tension in the neck, often caused by a chronic avoidance of turning the head to listen, which may have inhibited our ability to perceive sound. The Elephant restores natural flexibility to the neck. It also integrates the left and right sides of the brain for increased ability to listen and comprehend and for increasing short and long term-memory.

The Footflex

Sit in a chair and rest your left ankle on top of your right knee. Form a V with your left hand and place it on both sides of the back of the calf muscle right below the back of the left knee. Place the right hand on both sides of the Achilles tendon, about an inch or two above the left leg's anklebone. At both locations, while you are grasping the muscle, begin to pull your fingers apart. This will give a slight stretch to the back of the calf muscle. Continue this pulling while you point and flex the left foot up and down for thirty seconds. Don't move your foot side to side or in a circle. Just move it up and down.

Repeat with the right ankle on the left knee.

Explanation: The Footflex restores the natural length of the tendons in the calf area. It relaxes the reflex desire to hold back which increases our abilities to communicate, concentrate, lead, and complete tasks.

The Grounder

The Grounder is similar to a fencing lunge movement. Stand with your legs a comfortable distance apart—as though you are going to do a split. Point your right foot toward the right. Keep your left foot pointing forward. Now bend your right knee as you exhale, keeping the left leg straight. Keep your hips facing squarely forward. Protect the right knee by bending no further than the middle of the right foot.

Repeat three times and then repeat it in the other direction, keeping the right leg straight and bending the left knee.

Explanation: The Grounder lengthens and relaxes the hips, which stabilizes the balance of the body. This increases comprehension, short-term memory, self-expression, and organizational skills including doing phone and desk work.

The Owl

Take your left hand and with the thumb and fingers grasp the right shoulder muscle near the neck that runs along the top of the shoulder. Squeeze the muscle firmly and lift it slightly with your left hand. Inhale and turn your head to look back over your right shoulder. Now as you exhale, rotate your head to the left side, to look back over the left shoulder. Do this rotation a total of three times and then drop your chin to your chest while you relax your shoulder muscle.

Repeat using the right hand on the left shoulder.

Explanation: The Owl releases tension in the shoulder and neck muscles. This restores range of motion for turning the head and increases the circulation of blood and energy, which improves listening comprehension as well as thinking, speaking abilities and the use of a computer.

The Positive Points

Just above the center of both eyebrows and halfway up to the hairline, you will find a slight bump where the head curves. Place three fingers together lightly on the bumps. Close your eyes and breathe.

Hold the points for thirty seconds to one minute.

Explanation: The Positive Points are acupressure points for diffusing the fight-or-flight reflex, which releases emotional stress related to specific memories. Holding these points will also release temporary memory blocks and increase your ability to hear other points of view. It will allow you to give a presentation in a more relaxed manner.

The Thinking Cap

Using both hands simultaneously, start at the top of each ear by placing the index and middle fingers together behind the curved part of the ear. With the thumb at the front of the ear, begin to "unroll" the curved part of the edge of the ear by pulling the thumb back and flattening the curved part of the ear. Continue all the way to the bottom of the ear.

Repeat this a total of three times.

Explanation: The Thinking Cap helps the brain tune out distracting sounds and noises and tune into meaningful rhythms and sounds. This movement increases listening ability, short-term memory, and abstract thinking skills.

CHAPTER 5

CALIBRATION

There is one more process to learn before we put it all together and do a complete Brain Gym Balance and it is called Calibration. Calibration is helpful for two reasons: 1) on its own, Calibration prepares your body and mind for learning new information, and 2) when done before Muscle Checking with a Partner, Self Muscle Checking, or Noticing, Calibration aligns your mind-body system to achieve more accurate results.

I call this procedure Calibration because it correlates to calibration in a scientific setting. When two pieces of scientific equipment are used in the same experiment, they are first adjusted or calibrated to each other so the readings are consistent. This assures that both pieces of equipment are measuring the same levels. If researchers don't calibrate the equipment before they begin the experiment, they have no way of knowing if their results are accurate. This relates to the Brain Gym work because—just like the pieces of equipment in the scientific experiment—it is possible for the body-mind to be out of sync in a way that will cause inaccurate responses. For example, if you are doing Muscle Checking with a Partner and *either* the person being checked or the person doing the checking is not in calibration to the other, you may get inaccurate responses from the person being checked.

Let's say you are doing the process of Muscle Checking with a Partner with a partner named Susan. If you muscle check her on the statement, "My name is Susan," and she muscle checks "no," you obviously have an inappropriate response. That means that something in her system or in your system is causing an imbalance that led to this inappropriate response. This can be prevented if both of you do the calibration procedure before you do the muscle checking. Calibration can also be used while you are in the middle of a Balance session. Let's say the person being balanced starts to have inappropriate responses, such as being switched-off to something that clearly should be switched-on. Just stop the Balance and do another round of Calibration and then proceed with the Balance.

If you are using Self Muscle Checking or Noticing for your biofeedback response method, and therefore don't have a partner to calibrate with, the process of Calibration is still helpful because it will prepare you internally so your mind-body is ready and able to learn.

Calibration allows us to confidently rely on the results of the biofeedback response method we are using. There are two ways to do Calibration. There is a fast, easy way, which is presented below. This method is in the instructions for each of the Balances in this book. And, for those who want more details, there is a more comprehensive calibration process, which also explains the underlying validation behind each of the steps. This more extensive version of Calibration is presented in Appendix A on page 239. If you prefer, you can substitute the version in Appendix A whenever you are asked to do the Calibration procedure.

In the Calibration procedure below I'll explain the purpose of each of the parts. Then, beginning on page 76 you will find the condensed procedure for doing each step in Calibration.

Part 1: Water and Hydration

Water is the most important liquid you can put into your body. About 60 to 70 percent of your body is water and it is the one liquid you must absolutely have, in one form or another, to live. Of course, many of us already know about the necessity of drinking eight glasses of water a day. But what many of us do not know is exactly why we need so much water.

Your body must be sufficiently hydrated so it can send the chemical and electrical signals needed in order to perform both mentally and physically. If you are dehydrated, these signals will be interfered with which will interfere with a myriad of bodily functions, including:

- As a major component of blood, water is part of the delivery system that carries oxygen to the brain and each cell in the body.
- The digestive system uses several gallons of water daily to process food.
- Water is crucial for the lymphatic system, which is responsible for carrying away waste products.
- Because it ionizes cell salts in the body, water has a major role in producing the electrolytes that are necessary for the electrical activity to occur across the membranes of your cells.
- Every joint in your body requires water as a lubricant so that your movements will be smooth and painless.
- Your brain, which is about three-quarters water, requires sufficient hydration to perform all of the chemical reactions that are required to run the body.

The feeling of thirst in your mouth is slightly ahead of the body's need for water. By the time you begin to feel thirsty, you are moving into in a state of dehydration. Even a small loss of water will have serious consequences, including a laboratory-proven measurable decrease in physical performance. This negative impact occurs when you lose a mere two percent of your total body water, which is equivalent to the average amount lost at the end of an hour of exercise. If your water loss amounts to somewhere between six and seven percent, you will experience definite symptoms of dehydration and weakness. When you exercise if you rely solely on thirst to remind you to replenish water, it may take your body a full 24 hours after a workout to return to proper hydration levels.

Even as you sit and read this page, your body is maintaining a constant, light perspiration. The amount of perspiration increases as you experience stress or undergo more strenuous activities. You also lose water in the form of vapor every time you exhale. Both air conditioning and heat cause additional dehydration of your body. On a typical day, you excrete two and one-half quarts of water from your body. And if you exercise for an hour or more or live in a dry climate, you could lose up to an additional quart.

When exercising, even a mild degree of dehydration can affect your performance. Here are some guidelines to make sure that doesn't happen when you exercise[14]:

- Drink 8 ounces of water before exercising.
- Drink approximately 4 ounces of water every 15 minutes or so while exercising.
- Drink eight ounces of water twenty to thirty minutes after you finish exercising.

Herbal teas and watered-down fruit juices and sports drinks can be counted toward your water intake. But beverages that contain caffeine, such as coffee, tea, and some sodas, have a diuretic effect and actually remove fluid from the body. This means for every cup of caffeinated beverage you drink, only two-thirds of it can be counted towards your water intake for the day.

Simply sipping water throughout the day is a way for you to maintain your mental fitness. It may also help reduce the amount of fatigue you feel on days when you've drunk a lot of caffeinated drinks.

To complete this part of Calibration, simply drink some water.

Part 2:   Electrical Circuitry

To get in Calibration for electrical circuitry, which is designed to make sure electrical signals are flowing through the body, do Brain Buttons in Chapter 4 on page 61.

Part 3:   Activating

In this part of Calibration, you are switching your system into gear for doing the physical Brain Gym movements. You are activating your body to move. To do this, do The Cross Crawl in Chapter 4 on page 65.

Part 4:   Stress Reduction

The Stress Reduction aspect of Calibration is designed to dial down your adrenal glands if they are over-stimulated. If the

---

14 Guidelines for water needs during exercise from a study by Evian Water.

adrenal glands are secreting adrenalin, then your body is in a "fight-or-flight" modality, which is a survival state. In this mode, it changes the circuitry and the operation of the entire body and you are not able to learn new information or fully experience new situations. To make sure the stress response is not activated, simply do the Brain Gym movement called Hook-ups in Chapter 4 on page 63.

Part 5: Method to Use

If you are working without a partner and using a Noticing or Self Muscle Checking method as your biofeedback response, just determine the Noticing or Self Muscle Checking method you will be using. (See pages 45 to 54.)

If you are working with a partner, do the Muscle Checking for Normal response with a hard or light pressure, which you learned in Chapter 3. (See page 39.) If you are working with a partner, it's important to do this step so you get the feel for your partner's level of resistance. It's also the opportunity for the person who is being muscle checked to give you feedback, especially if the pressure is too hard for his arm.

Part 6: "Yes"/"No" Response

Do Muscle Checking with a Partner, Self Muscle Checking or Noticing for "yes" or "no" responses on both of the following statements:

- "My body will demonstrate for me a 'Yes' response." (With Light or Heavy Pressure Checking your arm should stay up.)
- "My body will demonstrate for me a 'No' response." (With Light or Heavy Pressure Checking your arm should go down.)

When you have completed the Calibration process you should get appropriate responses to both of these statements—switched-on for the "yes" and switched-off for the "no." With Self Muscle Checking and Noticing observe the difference in response between the "yes" and "no" responses.

Now that you understand the concept, here are the step-by-step instructions for doing Calibration in a Balance.

Calibration Procedure

1. **Water and Hydration:** To make sure you well hydrated, drink some water.
2. **Electrical Circuitry:** To make sure your electrical circuitry is operating efficiently, do Brain Buttons (page 61).
3. **Activating:** To make sure your body is ready to move, do The Cross Crawl (page 65).
4. **Stress Reduction:** To make sure your stress response is deactivated, do Hook-ups (page 63).
5. **Biofeedback Method to Use:** Select whether you will do Muscle-Checking with a Partner, Self Muscle Checking, or Noticing (pages 39 to 54). (View online muscle checking demonstrations at www.SwitchedOnNetworking.com/demo.)
6. **"Yes/No" Response:** Use the biofeedback response method you chose to ask the body for a "yes" and then a "no" response. See page 45.

NOTE: When you are in the middle of a Balance, you may begin to get inaccurate or questionable results. While this rarely occurs, it is possible and, in case it does, I want you to know what to do about it. Simply repeat the Calibration procedure, and then proceed with the Balance, beginning at the same point where you started to get the inaccurate results.

CHAPTER 6

THE BRAIN GYM BALANCES

Now we're ready to put all the pieces together and learn how to do a Brain Gym Balance.[15] It is the Balance that will actually re-educate the brain, allowing you to discover the specific aspects of networking that are challenging and then *eliminate the internal blockage related to those challenges.* After doing the Balance, your brain will no longer perceive the blockage and, without effort, you will achieve greater success with your networking.

Dr. Dennison, who developed Brain Gym, explains a Balance like this: "Balancing, a term to which we in Educational Kinesiology gave a new meaning, refers to the entire Brain Gym process, including having a specific goal for each session; performing the action you're intending to improve (or some activity symbolic of same); experiencing the joy of movement; and noticing what works for you."[16]

As I mentioned earlier, you can think of a Brain Gym Balance as re-wiring and rebalancing the circuitry of your brain from a *fear / survival focus,* which is triggered by past negative or stressful experiences, to a *present time / choice focus.* Through this re-wiring process, you will create new neural pathways that will make it easier to achieve the success you are looking for in your career.

You may recall the discussion about the part of the brain called the amygdala in Chapter 1 (see page 18). In most cases, the goals that you find difficult to achieve are triggering an automatic stress response in the amygdala. This response causes your amygdala to send a signal to the body's fight-or-flight survival mechanism, which keeps you in the

---

15 The Brain Gym Balances used in *Switched-On Selling* are a variation of Brain Gym Balances as taught by Brain Gym International.
16 Dennison, page 45.

old "it's difficult to achieve" or "I can't do that" mental programming of that aspect of networking. You are caught up in the memory of negative experiences and stuck in your inability to achieve your goal. The Balance reprograms the brain so the signal will be directed to the cerebrum instead, allowing you to choose a new response related to that situation. By doing the Balances, you will be *switching off* the amygdala's stress response while you will be *switching on* the cerebrum's ability to choose new responses for the different aspects of networking.

For example, if a person who is uncomfortable networking with people at an industry event does a Balance for being able to easily and effortlessly connect with people, the amygdala will no longer bring up the old programming that made it difficult and uncomfortable. The Balance changes the wiring in the amygdala, allowing the cerebrum to now take over and respond with new, positive programming. After doing the Balance, she will find it much easier to connect with others. In fact, she may even find it enjoyable—even when she's meeting a lot of new people.

So now let's look at what happens in a Brain Gym Balance:

1. First, after you've read through each of Donna's chapters, you'll be able to check Donna's Main Points as to whether you are switched-on or off for them.

2. Next, you'll be able to identify if there are any additional points that Donna raised that you found stressful as you were reading it. These are what I call Trigger Points. They show up as a small inner voice or feeling that says, "I can't do what Donna says to do in this aspect of networking." For example, your Trigger Point issue might be, "When I call someone to network I get nervous and stumble over my words." After you write the Trigger Point down, write a positive statement in the column next to it. In writing this positive statement allow yourself to see you solving or successfully doing whatever it was that triggered you, even if you don't believe it yet. Using the example above, you might write "I am calm, confident, and clear when I place a call to network with someone."

3. You'll use Muscle Checking with a Partner, Self Muscle Checking, or Noticing to check both the Trigger Point that you wrote and the positive statement. At this point, you should be switched-off for both.

4. Next, you'll do a physical role play or action for twenty seconds or so to represent each of the statements that are switching you off in Donna's Main Points and the Trigger Points section. While I know some people feel awkward doing this "role play," it is important to do because it activates areas of the brain that are involved with the physical aspects of networking. Doing the role play will determine whether you are switched off when you physically make believe you are doing the activity. You'll determine if you are switched-on or off for each action.

5. The fifth step will be for you to determine if you will include past events that relate to the current situation in this Balance.

6. The sixth step will be for you to do all Brain Gym movements and exercises listed in that step in the chapter. These movements and exercises are what will integrate your entire system for the goal.

7. The seventh step will be for you to go through *all* the statements again—both Donna's Main Points and your Trigger Point positive statements to confirm that you are switched-on for all of them.

8. Next, you'll repeat the physical role play or action *only for the actions you had been switched-off for the first time through the Balance.*

9. *If you have a partner, you will celebrate your success. If you were doing Self Muscle Checking or Noticing, give yourself a big pat on the shoulder.*

10. *Finally, if this was the only balance you are doing at this point, you'll check the Home Play section (see page 231). If you are doing other balances during this session, you'll wait until you have done the last one to go to the Home Play section.*

NOTE: Each Balance is presented with step-by-step instructions, so you don't have to remember the steps.

As you go through a chapter, it is possible that you will find that you are switched-on for all of the statements in that chapter. In other words, none of Donna's Main Points switched you off. And you had no additional Trigger Point issues come up for you as you read through that chapter. This means that you don't have any difficulties or issues with this aspect of networking. If you find that's the case, you will go directly to the Brain Gym exercises and movements in that section. Even though you are already switched-on for the topics that were covered in that chapter, by doing the Brain Gym exercises you may strengthen your abilities related to that specific area of networking. If you are already good in this area you may move to being great and even more successful.

The Steps to a Brain Gym Balance

Now you are ready to do your first complete Balance, the Balance for Positive Networking. Then, in Part II (Chapters 7 through 13), you'll find Donna's networking strategies for the following additional aspects of networking, coupled with the Balance specifically designed for each of these topics:

- Fulfilling Your Goals With Networking
- Effective People Skills
- Nurturing Your Network
- Connecting Online and Face-to-Face
- Upgrading Your Conversations
- Networking as a Time-Saver
- Being a Prosperous Networker

Having a Positive Networking Attitude

Let's begin this part of the process with Donna sharing with you how to create a networking attitude that produces positive results.

Identify Statements for Balance Section:

As you read through Donna's information in this chapter, be aware of any issues that surface in your mind. For example, in Donna's upcoming section, at one point she talks about what it's like when someone calls and asks you for a favor. For some people, reading that might bring up an immediate discomfort or negative thought. It's those feelings and thoughts that we're re-wiring and rebalancing with the Balance for a Positive Networking Attitude. For the purpose of the exercise at the end of the chapter, you will be thinking of and focusing on a negative past networking situation. That's what you'll focus on when you get to the Balance.

So... here's Donna!

One thing that I notice about masterful networkers is that their "networking" is such an integrated, natural aspect of who they are that it's transparent. When they network, you never really notice that they're networking. And yet, what I do notice is that they accomplish big goals easily with the support of others, they get their phones calls returned quickly, and magical synchronicities seem to happen regularly in their lives.

Sometimes there is a misconception that to be a powerful networker you have to be aggressive and "on" all the time. And yet, the most effective networkers are the ones who truly enjoy connecting with people and enjoy the experience of being a resource and contributing to the success of others. If networking feels like work to you, if you feel like you have to "be on" to network, if you feel like you're being manipulative, if you relate to networking as a technique that you only use when there's something you want from others, then you're not really networking. Networking is not a technique; it's a way of relating, connecting, and creating a community of support.

What Networking IS and What It's NOT

- Networking is *not* about manipulating. It's about requesting information and contacts so that you can accomplish your goals

81

with more ease, fun, and efficiency.
- Networking is *not* about working hard. It is about working smart by accessing the resources all around you.
- And networking is certainly *not* about "being on" all the time unless "being on" for you means being present with people while having fun connecting and sharing resources in an easy, natural manner.

If you're working hard at networking, you will **not** enjoy meeting people and you will not be fun to be with. Relax, enjoy, have fun! The more at ease you are when talking with people—and remember networking simply happens through conversation—the more people will enjoy being with you. Your attitude, your focus and your approach are key ingredients to experience networking as a fun, fulfilling way to be with people.

Just think about the word "networking." A *net* is an interlocking system of some kind and the word *working* means "to function, to operate." When your net is working, your "interconnected group of people" are functioning by interacting with each other so that resources, support, and ideas are being passed throughout the network to the people who can gain benefit from the information, ideas, and support.

Ideally, networking is a fun approach to connecting with people and accomplishing results. And when you're networking and contributing to the success of others, you experience the satisfaction and fulfillment that is a natural part of the networking process.

Your Attitude Affects You and Others

Some people say that attitude is everything. And if you've ever been around someone with a sour attitude, you will probably agree. Just as being with someone who has an unpleasant attitude can be draining, being with someone who has a light, fun attitude can be a joy. Your attitude influences your thoughts, feelings, behaviors, and results— while at the same time influencing the people around you.

Your attitude is important when networking because it affects the way you relate, react, and respond to people—the way you feel about yourself and the way you approach others. If you have a strong sense of self and a healthy awareness of your strengths and weaknesses, you will tend to feel more comfortable asking for and offering support.

Your attitude affects both the way people respond to you and the way you experience other people. Your attitude can turn people off or be a positive signal for people to interact with you. A positive attitude toward yourself and others will help you develop a natural networking style where it is easy and comfortable to meet people, make contacts, and build strong relationships.

Just like the background music of a movie sets the tone for the scenes and emotions being portrayed, your attitude sets the tone for your interactions and your life. It takes only a simple shift in attitude to change or enhance your life. Your attitude is your choice. You can at any moment realize your attitude is not in sync with what you choose for your life and then make a new choice.

Attitude Check

What is your attitude when someone calls and asks for a favor?
- "What does he want now?"
- "Why hasn't he called before now?"
- "I sure am glad he thought to call me so that I can help."
- "It sure is good to hear from him. I would like to stay more in touch."
- "That was pretty impressive of him to call. I admire what he is up to."

Each of these statements reflect a different way of responding to the same phone call, running the gamut from a negative attitude to a positive one. If you look at each of these possibilities and imagine what a person would likely say, do, and think based on that attitude, it's fairly easy to see how it would influence the conversation—or lack of conversation—and the potential for a positive networking experience.

How about when someone approaches you at a networking event? What is your attitude then?
- "Oh no, here comes someone who probably wants to sell me something."
- "I don't know what to say ... what is she going to think of me?"
- "Here's someone new for me to meet. Let's see who she is."
- "I'm going to just relax and let myself enjoy meeting this person."

- "I sure hope this person needs my product. I want to get a new client tonight."

Obviously, these are very different responses to the same exact situation. Imagine how this scenario might play out for you. What would your body language be like? What words, actions, and thoughts might come to your mind? And what would it lead to?

In each of the above scenarios, which of the examples most closely resembles the attitude that you tend to have in that situation? Is there another attitude that you would prefer and that would be more beneficial? If so, identify how you can adopt that attitude while also identifying the way you would look, act, and behave as a result of having that attitude.

Attitude Adjustments

What you say and think conveys your attitude. So start noticing your thoughts and comments about networking so that you can then consciously choose an attitude that incorporates networking easily and effectively. Here are some examples for you to consider:

"They probably don't have time."
becomes
"I call on people in a way that respects their time."
or
"I respectfully approach people to request time with them."

* * * * * *

"I can do this myself."
becomes
"I work efficiently and effectively with others."
or
"I appreciate how much more effective I can be with the support of my network."

* * * * * *

"I know what needs to be done here."
becomes
"I know I have people in my network who can provide me with valuable information."
or
"I am receptive to ideas and suggestions that enhance my plans."

* * * * * *

"I don't want to bother people."
becomes
"I make clear requests of people in my network and approach them with respect and appreciation for their time and energy.

* * * * * *

"I don't know them well enough to call."
becomes
"I get to know people better by calling them and networking with them."

* * * * * *

"They probably don't know anyone who…"
becomes
"The best way to find out is to ask."

Pass It On Attitude

The best way to have a fully functioning, active network is to give generously and establish a flow of support and information. You are a wealth of information, ideas, and contacts. And the value of your network is for all of that information, all of those ideas, and all of those contacts to be passed around to one another for the good of everyone. Think of networking as a form of recycling. Use the information, ideas and contacts that come to you in whatever way is of value to you and then pass it on.

Giving is an effective way to activate your network because it is a basic human nature to respond in kind. Think about it: When someone does something for you, you instinctually desire to give back. When people have a "pass it on" attitude, giving creates a flow within their network. Giving and contributing to one another becomes second nature and makes life even more interesting and fun.

To "Pass It On" means "I graciously receive the value of what is given to me and then pass along the information/value to someone else." I like to think of giving as a guaranteed process for reciprocity. The guarantee of giving is what I call the "boomerang effect" of networking. A boomerang always comes back because it is designed to do so. In the same way, what you give always comes back in some form because that is the design of the law of giving and thus the law of networking. However, the boomerang can't return unless someone takes action and throws it out in the first place. So get your "giving power" into action by passing support and information along to others. Then watch for that boomerang and catch it on its return.

Get in the habit of being a resource. When some new information comes across your desk or into your social network, ask yourself:

- Now who else would be interested in this?
- Who else would get value from this?
- Who else would relate to this in a productive way?

In order to pass along opportunities to people in your network, find out their goals and aspirations. Once you know what's important to them, you can feed them with meaningful contacts and resources that align with their goals. When first meeting people, get to know as much as you can about them and their business/job so that you will discover what information, ideas, and contacts you have that can be of value to them. This is not about "spoon feeding" someone, it's more like giving them a recipe. It's up to the people in your network to follow through and make productive use of any information, ideas, and contacts that you give them. Your part is to give them the input and enjoy watching them grow as a result of your support and their actions.

When a masterful networker encounters a new person or new online community, she doesn't just think about what's in it for her. Instead, she asks herself, "How can I be a resource?" "How can I be of service" and "What do I have to offer here?" Whether you're meeting someone new or talking with someone you already know, ask yourself:

- Who can I recommend who would be a beneficial resource for her?
- What similar jobs, projects, or situations have I been in where I

learned something that could be of value to him?
- What can I say that will be encouraging, empowering, and/or supportive?

Inclusive Attitude

Networking is about shifting from *me* to *we*. Thinking only of yourself limits your outreach and effectiveness in life. You may have been very conditioned by our culture to think you should be strong and independent—and not require anyone's support. However, it is unrealistic to think that we don't need the support of others. You actually depend on thousands of people to grow, harvest, and transport food to the grocery store in your neighborhood so that you never have to worry about having food within easy access. You depend on thousands of people to design, develop, and build the thousands of products that you use in your home, office, and cars every day.

We are a network of people working independently and collaboratively to provide products, services, and resources that are important in people's lives. Networking links people to one another for the mutual benefit of everyone involved. Networking is choosing interdependence over isolation and realizing the power of cooperation over competition.

The "I can do it on my own" mentality limits your outreach and effectiveness as a networker. Life is more fun and your success can be greater than you ever imagined when you shift to the mental state of "I honor the power and results that are accomplished from working effectively with others."

"Tell Me More" Attitude

Think about how you feel when someone truly shows an interest in you, your business, your hobbies. Being interested and curious, in a positive way, about someone is validating and affirming. Curiosity means "desire to know or learn." When you have the desire to get to know someone and learn about their life and their business, you are more likely to generate an interesting conversation. Your curiosity will have you focus on other people, be more attentive, and listen more closely. As a result, people will be more likely to connect with you and share more information with you.

Children have a natural curiosity. When they see other children their age, they often gravitate to each other and start playing together before you know it. What if adults operated with the same curiosity, freedom, and spontaneity? Imagine walking into a room and simply seeing a bunch of new "playmates." You're not sure what fun business games you might decide to "play," but you know that you are ready to have fun connecting with people. Instead of approaching people with fears or shoulds, you are brimming over with curiosity about what might develop when you approach new people at a networking event and are ready to make connections that enhance your networking efforts.

Being interested in people will also help to diminish any tendency you might have to be judgmental. After all, it's possible that a snap judgment about a person or a situation might close us off from the best connection we've ever made. From a mindset of curiosity, it's easier to let go of your negative thoughts about others and be more accepting of them as they are.

One caution: Don't go overboard with curiosity to the point of coming across as an interrogator. Be curious and interested—not from a place of being nosey—but from a place of interest and making a connection.

Here are some examples of using a "Tell Me More" Attitude:

- "Tell me more about ...."
- "I am interested in how you got into this business."
- "The way you describe what you do is interesting because ...."
- "I am interested in knowing how I can be of support."
- "I am curious about how you first got interested in ...."

Personal Touch Attitude

Being professional, while at the same time providing a personal touch, can make the difference in creating new business relationships that turn into long-term networking relationships. My friend Addis certainly found that to be true when her brokerage company handed over some clients to her who had not been serviced very well by the former broker. One couple felt strongly that the former broker had, in fact, "dropped the ball" and they were therefore skeptical about working with another broker from the same company. They were frustrated with brokers getting their business and then not showing the interest, or making the effort to develop a long-term client/broker relationship.

Although Addis does fee-based work, this particular couple wouldn't commit to paying a fee. Addis worked with them for four months for nothing in an attempt to be of service and establish some trust and build the relationship. She did retirement plan reports and helped them get an attorney for estate planning. Then one day on the phone Addis heard their dog barking in the background. Something clicked for Addis and she decided to send the dog, Molly, two dog toys. The wife, who had always been very reserved and quiet in all of their meetings and interactions, was impressed and thrilled. She later told Addis that she had been telling all of her friends that their broker had sent Molly some toys. In their subsequent interactions, this client repeatedly told Addis how considerate she was: "Every time we see Molly playing with those toys, we think of you. That was so thoughtful."

Who would have thought that sending toys to their dog would have made the difference in developing the necessary trust and rapport for a successful relationship? Sending toys to a client's dog may seem like such a simple—and possibly even a silly thing—to do. Yet, prior to Addis, this couple had broker after broker who made no attempt to build a relationship with them. They had never had anyone show any interest in anything other than investing their money. Finally someone showed up who noticed who they were as a couple and even paid attention to their dog.

This couple signed up with Addis and she made sure to stay in touch with them—and their dog—on a regular basis to stay connected with them regarding their financial goals.

Adventurous Attitude

Helen Keller said, "Life is either a daring adventure or nothing." You could say the same thing about networking, "Networking is either a daring adventure or nothing." When you approach networking as an adventure, you maintain enthusiasm, expectancy, and open-mindedness. An adventure implies that you are on a certain path and yet you don't always know what is going to come your way along that path. However, an adventure is typically pursued with excitement and anticipation of some good things to happen along the path that you have chosen and a willingness to overcome any perceived obstacles.

Networking is like a "Treasure Hunt." When you are on a treasure hunt, you know there are "jewels" out there, you just don't know where. The fun is finding the jewels. The same is true with networking; there are jewels out there everywhere. You just don't know where. The adventure of networking is that "you never know" where a new job, client, partner, employee, or friend may come from. And that's why it's so important to pay attention to the people around you.

Networking is a process for discovering opportunities that may be only one person, one phone call, one online posting, or one conversation away. So you meet this person, talk to that person, join a social media site, go to a meeting, call another person, post a message online—and sometimes nothing will happen. Then, all of a sudden, you'll find one of those jewels. And sometimes those jewels show up in the most unexpected places. That's the fun of a treasure hunt. You never know who you might meet that will become a great connection for you. Imagine your life as a treasure hunt! Enjoy the treasures. Allow it to be fun. Enjoy the experience and I guarantee you'll have a life full of jewels.

BALANCE FOR A POSITIVE NETWORKING ATTITUDE

You are now ready to learn how to do a Balance.

In Step 1 of the Balance for a Positive Networking Attitude you will do Calibration. In Step 2 you will pick a negative networking situation to focus on. It may be from what was triggered in the information you read in Donna's section above. Did a negative thought come up? For this Balance you can also pick a negative networking situation you've experienced in the past. It could be about a time you felt uncomfortable walking into a room full of people or a situation where you didn't call someone because you didn't want to bother them. Any memory of an unpleasant networking experience from your past can continue to negatively influence your networking effectiveness—until you do a Balance.

What this Balance will do is literally remove the negative charge attached to that experience from your brain in two minutes. You'll still have access to the memory of this situation but it will no longer have a negative impact when you bring it to mind. Sounds miraculous, doesn't it? The fact is that when you have completed the process and you think of the original thought, it will be like you are reading about it in a novel. You will no longer carry the "negative charge," so thinking about it will no longer be a stress.

STEP 1. CALIBRATION: Preparation for Balancing Process

If necessary, refer to the more detailed instructions on Calibration on page 71.

1. **Water and Hydration:** To make sure you are well hydrated, drink some water.
2. **Electrical Circuitry:** To make sure your electrical circuitry is operating efficiently, do Brain Buttons (page 61).
3. **Activating:** To make sure your body is ready to move, do The Cross Crawl (page 65).
4. **Stress Reduction:** To make sure your stress response is deactivated, do Hook-ups (page 63).
5. **Method to Use:** Select whether you will do Muscle-Checking with a Partner, Self Muscle Checking or Noticing (pages 39 to 54). (View online muscle checking demonstrations at www.SwitchedOnNetworking.com/demo.)
6. **"Yes/No" Response:** Use the biofeedback response method you chose to ask the body for a "yes" and then a "no" response (page 45).

NOTE: When you are in the middle of a Balance, it's possible you may begin to get inaccurate or questionable results. While this rarely occurs, it is a possibility. In case it does occur, simply repeat the Calibration procedure, and then proceed with the Balance, beginning at the point where you began to experience the inaccurate or questionable results.

Let's now have you experience the next steps to the process.

STEP 2. IDENTIFYING TRIGGER POINTS FOR YOURSELF:

Pick a negative situation that was triggered by reading Donna's strategies or, if nothing she shared in this section triggered you, pick a negative networking situation that recently happened to you or a situation from your past that still bothers you.

STEP 3. CHECKING THE ISSUE: Visualization

In this step, picture in your mind the situation you selected in Step 2. Focus on the negative aspect of it. Once you have it fully visualized in your mind, do Muscle-Checking with a Partner, Self Muscle Checking or Noticing.
Are you Switched-On or Switched-Off?
In almost all cases, because you picked a negative or stressful situation, you will be switched-off and your arm will come down. If this is did not occur, then pick another negative or stressful situation to use for this Balance so that your response is switched-off. Next, proceed to Step 4.

STEP 4. CHOOSING TO INCLUDE THE PAST

In a moment you will be saying out loud to yourself (or to your partner, if you are working with a partner):

"My system now incorporates, in the most appropriate way, all relevant past events, known and unknown, into the Step 3 experience."

Let me explain the purpose of the Step 4 statement before you do Muscle-Checking with a Partner, Self Muscle Checking or Noticing. In effect, you are asking your mind-body if there are any negative events that happened earlier in your life that relate to the current situation you visualized in Step 3.

Here's an example. Perhaps someone you telephoned responded to your networking request in a way that caused you to feel dismissed or rejected. The triggering event that caused you to feel rejected might have occurred when you were six years old when someone was negative to you when you were on the phone. This memory is still stored in the part of the brain called the amygdala. (See page 18.) The amygdala will receive the electrical signal from the words spoken. As part of its job, the amygdala is looking for a memory of when something negative happened to you when you were on the phone. When the amygdala finds that time when you were six years old, it then sends a signal to trigger the adrenal glands to secrete adrenalin, which subconsciously puts the body back in that same feeling of rejection.

The statement you're reading out loud is asking your amygdala if there is something from the past stored there. If your system finds something, you are asking if it wants to get rid of that past trigger (or triggers if there is more than one past situation similar to the current situation) during the current Balance.

In effect a "yes" response means the body is saying that I have triggers from the past on this subject in the amygdala and my body does want to discharge them during this Balance.

If you are Noticing, just observe if it feels as if there is something from the past involved with the current situation. If it feels like there is, you can simply choose to incorporate it into the current Balance. If you are Self Muscle Checking or using Muscle Checking with a Partner, then a "Yes" response means your amygdala has some triggers from the past on this subject stored in it and your body will include them in the current Balance even if you don't know exactly what the situation or situations are in your conscious mind.

Note: If you get a "No" response, it is not wrong. It simply means either there is nothing in your past related to this current situation or that the situation is not something that your system wants to deal with at the present time.

Now do Muscle-Checking with a Partner, Self Muscle Checking or Noticing and you'll get either a "yes" or "no" response on this statement: "My system now incorporates, in the most appropriate way, all relevant past events, known and unknown, into the Step 3 experience."

Whether you get a "yes" or a "no," continue on to Step 5.

STEP 5: TAKING ACTION: Doing the Brain Gym Movements

Now's the time for you to do the Brain Gym Movements listed below to create the rewiring impact on your body and your mind which will get rid of the negative charge attached to your thoughts. This means when you are done with the Balance, the Trigger Point or the negative thought you selected in Step 3 will no longer be operating and controlling your thoughts and actions!

- Do Hook-ups (see page 63).
- Do The Positive Points (see page 69).

It should take approximately 1 to 2 minutes to do these two Brain Gym movements.

STEP 6. CHECKING THE CHANGES: Visualization

Picture the same situation as you did in Step 3 above. When you have the visual of the situation focused, do Muscle-Checking with a Partner, Self Muscle Checking or Noticing.

You should now be switched-on. The negative charge attached to that situation is gone. You can now think about the situation and it will not have a negative response.

STEP 7. WHERE ARE YOU NOW?

Now that you have switched off the negative charge attached to that networking situation and are switched-on, Notice: 1) what you observed happening while you were doing Hook-ups and The Positive Points and 2) how you feel when you think about the situation now. If you have a partner, share your observations with him. (*Hint:* You might have noticed that it became difficult to focus on the negative situation or that your mind wandered off when you attempted to think about it. If so, that's because the negative is no longer being activated.)

STEP 8. IT'S TIME TO CELEBRATE

If you're working with a partner, congratulate your partner on the successful completion of the Balance for Positive Selling. If you're Noticing or Self Muscle Checking, congratulate yourself.

Will This Last?

You have now removed the charge from this negative, stressful situation. You might now be thinking, "How long will this last?" Well, the negative stressful energy attached to this situation may be gone forever. If the trigger you focused on was related to what you read in Donna's material, you will now be able to do what she was talking about without being triggered.

However, if something re-triggers you, simply do Hook-ups and The Positive Points while thinking of the negative situation again to get rid of the charge. You can use this Balance for any negative, stressful networking situation that occurs. If your first networking interaction of the day is negative, do this Balance to immediately get rid of the charge so you can still create a positive networking day for yourself.

You're Ready to Proceed

This is the basic format you will be following for all of the other Balances in this book. You are now ready to incorporate Brain Gym into all aspects of the networking process. As I mentioned before, the rest of the book has been divided into seven categories—fulfilling your goals with networking, being an effective networker, nurturing your network, connecting online and face-to-face, upgrading your conversations, networking as a timesaver, and being a prosperous networker.

THE SWITCHED-ON NETWORKING QUESTIONNAIRE

Before we go further, we'd like you to fill out the Switched-On Networking Questionnaire. This will allow you to identify your current strong points in the networking process as well as your areas of difficulty. At the end of each Balance in the upcoming chapters, you'll have the opportunity to re-check what has changed for you. Please be honest when you are filling out the questionnaire so you will see clearly what has changed from doing the Balance process.

Place a check mark in the column that most clearly reflects your level of agreement or disagreement with each statement below:

		Strongly Disagree	Disagree	Doesn't Apply	Agree	Strongly Agree
1.	I accomplish my networking goals easily and effectively.					
2.	I feel confident and strong in making clear requests that support my personal and professional goals.					
3.	I am an effective networker.					
4.	I enjoy networking and being a resource for people.					
5.	I easily connect with people and build strong relationships.					
6.	I am inspired to be of service to others.					
7.	I enjoy nurturing my network by giving of my time and energy.					
8.	I am comfortable and confident acknowledging people and expressing my appreciation.					

		Strongly Disagree	Disagree	Doesn't Apply	Agree	Strongly Agree
9.	I know I am a valuable resource for others.					
10.	I am comfortable connecting with people through online and offline activities.					
11.	I am comfortable and confident attending networking events.					
12.	I feel confident and enjoy introducing myself to new people.					
13.	I easily and effectively develop my online presence.					
14.	I feel empowered when I speak.					
15.	I make clear and specific requests of others.					
16.	I easily choose words that can influence my network in a positive way.					
17.	I network efficiently, saving myself time and energy.					
18.	I am effective as a result of having a strong network of support.					
19.	My prosperity consciousness enhances my joy in sharing ideas and information with my network.					
20.	My network is a source of abundance in all areas of my life.					

PART II

NETWORKING STRATEGIES

BY DONNA FISHER

followed by
BRAIN GYM BALANCES

BY JERRY V. TEPLITZ, J.D., PH.D.

INTRODUCTION TO PART II

In this part of the book, Donna shares the networking perspectives and strategies that she has taught to individuals and groups across the United States. These networking strategies will help you break through to new dimensions in your career.

After each of Donna's sections, Jerry presents a Switched-On Networking Balance which is specifically targeted to that aspect of networking. As you read Donna's material, take note of the Trigger Point issues that surface in your mind.

When you find something in Donna's material that feels like a problem or challenge for you, go to the end of the chapter where the Balance is located and see if the problem or challenge is covered in the Step 2 part of the balance called CHECKING DONNA'S MAIN POINTS. If it is, then continue reading Donna's material. If your problem or challenge is not covered in the CHECKING DONNA'S MAIN POINTS section, then go to Step 3, IDENTIFYING TRIGGER POINTS FOR YOURSELF, and write down your Trigger Points in the space provided. Next to each of these Trigger Points, you'll rewrite it as a positive statement, as if you were able to accomplish it easily and effortlessly. Here's an example of a Trigger Point relating to networking and the Positive Goal Statement you might write next to it:

TRIGGER POINTS	POSITIVE GOAL STATEMENTS
Example: "When I walk into a room full of people, my palms start to sweat and I get nervous."	Example: "I am calm and confident when I walk into a room full of people."

You are now ready to cover the rest of the material in the book. Enjoy the journey!

CHAPTER 7

FULFILLING YOUR GOALS WITH NETWORKING

Identify Statements for Balance Section:

As you read through Donna's section below, be aware of any discomfort or negativity that comes to mind about the specific suggestions she makes. Make note of these responses and, when you get to the balance, if those issues are not covered, you'll have the opportunity to write them down.

Do you ever feel like your goals are simply out of reach? Or maybe sometimes you have difficulty imagining how you could accomplish your goals on your own.

Well, there's good news. You don't have to accomplish your goals on your own when you have a strong network of support. Your network can actually provide you with the stepping stones to reach your goals.

Many successful people will tell you that having clear goals and developing a strong network of support paved their path to success and the achievement of their financial dreams. When you are clear about the outcomes you choose to create in your life and you have a strong network of support, you can fulfill your accomplishments with more ease, fun, and efficiency.

Here are some ways to identify your highest choice outcomes and get on your own path to success.

1. Answer this question regarding all areas of your life, "What is my highest choice in life regarding …?"
   a. My career
   b. My family and relationships

    c. My health and well-being

    d. My finances

    e. My hobbies and recreational activities

    f. My own fulfillment—personal and spiritual

2. Brainstorm and notice which ideas, projects, and opportunities really excite and energize you.

3. Review your goals and ideal outcomes from the perspective of pursuing **your** heart's desire (rather than what you feel is expected of you).

4. Don't judge an idea as being too large or too small.

5. Continue to explore your own thoughts and feelings and clarify your direction by getting to the truth of the matter with the following questions:

    a. Am I *willing* to be who I have to be to fulfill this outcome?

    b. Am I *willing* to give up or change whatever has been in the way of accomplishing this goal?

    c. Am I *willing* take the actions that lead to this outcome?

    d. Is this goal in alignment with my top values and principles?

6. Ask yourself "What if… ?"

    a. What if I could have my best year ever?

    b. What if I could have a job that is both fulfilling and financially rewarding?

    c. What if this year I could fulfill my life-long desire to… ?

    d. What if I experienced an abundance of money, time, and support?

    e. What if… *[fill in the blank according to your heart's desire]*

7. Turn your "what if" answers into "I can," "I am," or "I will" statements.

    a. I *am* having my best year so far by …..

    b. This year I *choose to* find a job that is both fulfilling and financially rewarding.

    c. I *am* fulfilling my life-long desire to ….

By taking time to really explore your options and choices and discover deeply what matters to you, you will be able to get the most benefit from the Brain Gym processes that Jerry leads you through in this book. Identifying and telling the truth about what typically gets in the way of your success and creating clarity regarding your highest choice outcomes gives you the perfect information to allow the switched-on networking processes to make a major difference in your life. The Brain Gym balances will allow you to uncover your natural motivation so that you naturally take the actions that support your success.

Fulfillment Review

We tend to think of goals as something we have to work towards. And yet, a more empowering option is to think of your goals as outcomes fulfilled and then "begin with the end in mind" (a concept covered by Steven Covey in his book *Seven Habits of Highly Effective People*). The word "goal" implies somewhere to get to—while "outcome" represents a result already imagined as fulfilled. "Begin with the end in mind" and imagine your highest choice outcome already fulfilled. When you get in touch with your outcome fulfilled, then the ***who, what, where*** and ***when*** that will lead to your result becomes clear. As you fill in the blanks in the section below, step into an imagined state of fulfillment and imagine who assisted you, what actions you took, and how it feels to have your outcome fulfilled.

1. My highest choice outcome fulfilled is _____
   _____

2. The benefits of this outcome to me and my network are _____
   _____

3. Actions and behaviors that supported this outcome include:
   _____

4. My key supporters include: _____
   _____

5. My past tendencies to stop or sabotage myself were overcome
   by_____

6. My new agreements and new behaviors contributing to my success include: _____

7. I am efficient with my time and effective with my networking by_____

8. The daily actions that keep me on track include:

   _____

9. Experiencing my outcome fulfilled satisfies my values of

   _____

10. I gratefully celebrate my outcome fulfilled and reward myself by_____

11. My outcome fulfilled represents new opportunities for

   _____

When you experience the excitement and passion of having your outcomes fulfilled, you will have activated your energy, your imagination, your enthusiasm, and your direction. The clarity that this exercise brings will assist you in making more effective requests. You will also find that as new opportunities present themselves you will have more clarity regarding which opportunities to pursue.

Remember, everyone in your network knows someone who knows someone, who knows someone. Once you have identified your desired outcomes, think about the resources that can best serve you.

- Who are you interested in meeting who could assist you in accomplishing your goals?
- What organizations would be valuable for you to join based on your identified outcomes?
- What resources will you be calling on to support you in fulfilling on your outcomes?

Fulfillment in All Areas of Life

It is common for people to focus on networking as a business development tool, which it is. However, networking is also a life-enhancement system, a support system for creating fulfillment in all areas of your life.

I suggest using the chart below to easily and clearly identify people who are already in your network who have a similar interest or who are already accomplished in the area you are now focused on. List your goals as your "highest-choice outcomes" and then list the people who would be great supporters of your goals because of their expertise, talent, contacts, or interests. For example, in the category of "finances," you might list your CPA, banker, financial advisor, or a financially successful friend. In the area of health, you might include on your list people who eat healthy diets, exercise regularly, and cook nutritious meals. If necessary, use an extra sheet of paper.

	My Highest-Choice Outcomes	My Supporters from My Network
Career		
Health		
Finances		
Hobbies		
Relationships		
Spirituality		

Switched-on networkers easily and confidently ask for information, resources, and contacts because that's part of the process of networking—asking, collaborating, sharing, and utilizing available resources. Having clear goals makes your networking easy and natural. When you are in a conversation and someone mentions something that relates to your goals and outcomes, pay attention. Ask questions. Ask for more information. Ask for contacts.

It's Not About Rejection—So Reframe It!

When I am leading a networking workshop and I ask the attendees to write down the fears, concerns, and roadblocks that get in the way of networking, one of the concerns that shows up consistently is the fear of rejection.

And yet, networking is not about rejection. *The only way you can feel rejected is if you approach people with that state of mind.* The Brain Gym balances will assist you in stepping into your power so you can make requests of others without having a negative emotional charge if people are not responsive to your requests. When someone you call does not have what you are looking for, they are not rejecting you. They just don't happen to have what you're looking for. When someone does not take your call, they are not rejecting you. They may simply be busy on a project at that moment. When you are switched-on for making requests of others, you feel positive no matter how people respond because you have an inner resilience that empowers you. You can gain value from making requests whether people respond in your ideal way or not.

No matter how people respond to your requests, the value for you is:

1. You are *actively* engaged and creating results.
2. You gain greater insight into your ability to make *clear and compelling requests.*
3. You are connecting with people and *increasing your circle of friends.*
4. You can get valuable feedback that points you in a *new, positive direction.*
5. You are *making people aware of what you do*—even if they aren't resources for you at this time.

Ask—Ask—Ask!

Can you recall a situation when someone asked you for support and you felt honored, acknowledged, valued, and maybe even delighted to be able to be of support? Asking is an acknowledgement of the value and/or respect that you have for someone, because you certainly would not ask for help from someone if you did not value their advice or support.

We have a natural human desire to give, contribute, and be valued. A switched-on networker makes requests that acknowledge and inspire people to take positive action. And as a result the people in their network feel the satisfaction that comes from giving, contributing, and being valued by the people they know.

Even if it seems very obvious to you, don't assume that other people know how to support you. Asking for help and information is a way of including the people who are all around you and acknowledging them for the contribution or knowledge they have to share. Sometimes it is only because you ask that you gain access to information or contacts that open new doors of opportunity. Ask often.

Have you ever thought about contacting someone in your network for support or information and yet you didn't because of what I call "The Lone Ranger Mentality"? You know, thinking you should be able to do it all on your own! Well "The Lone Ranger Mentality" is a major mental roadblock to efficient networking. Instead of operating with a "Lone Ranger Mentality," *switch* your thinking and realize that "it takes a village" to create a success. And that "village" is your network.

Networking is the smart approach to success as you wisely access the resources available to you through your contacts. Since "asking" is the way you access those resources, here is a review of the empowering way to make a request.

Criteria for Asking
1. Be Clear
2. Be Concise
3. Be Specific
4. Be Non-demanding
5. Be Straightforward
6. Be Empowering

Let's a look at these criteria in more detail:

1. **Be Clear**

   Be clear about the resources, products, and/or services you are asking for so people don't have to spend time figuring out what you are asking for. The clearer you are, the more likely people are to respond at all—and to respond more quickly.

2. **Be Concise**

   Give enough information so people will understand what you are requesting but don't overload them with too much information. People can always ask questions if they desire more information. If you go on and on about what and why and how, you may lose their attention and miss out on an opportunity to get your desired response.

3. **Be Specific**

   Specific requests make it easier for people to go into their "mental computer" and search through their "files" to find the information you are requesting. Just like with a Google search, the more specific you are, the more likely you will access your information quickly and easily.

4. **Be Non-demanding**

   Make your request with no demands or no strings attached. By being gracious and non-demanding, you give people the chance to choose to give and experience the satisfaction that comes with contributing.

5. **Be Straightforward**

   Be straightforward so that there is no sense of manipulation, hype, exaggeration, or being put on the spot. When people experience that you are being honest and forthright, you are more likely to build a relationship based on respect.

6. **Be Empowering**

   Empower people by communicating how their assistance will make a difference. Ask with pride and have confidence in what you are asking people to support. Ask in such a way that people feel acknowledged and included. Thanking people for their assistance is also an empowering way to let them know you value their support.

Use the following examples to identify some empowering requests you can make of the people in your network:

- Who do you *recommend* _____
- Who do you know who would be helpful for me to know *given that* _____
- Who do you know who *knows* _____ _____
- Who do you know who *does* _____ _____
- I am interested in knowing who you suggest I talk with who has *experience with* _____
- I am *looking for* _____ , what do you recommend?
- What *ideas* would you be willing to share with me regarding __ _____

The words "recommend" and "suggest" are key because these words imply your sense of respect for the person's ideas and support. For example, in asking for a recommendation from within a person's company, you might say:

"I know there are other divisions of your company that conduct sales meetings and conferences. Who do you *recommend* I talk with about offering my networking presentations for your other corporate events around the country?"

Make your requests:
- *Inspiring* because you are up to "something"
- *Clear* because you know what to ask for
- *Satisfying* because people have an opportunity to feel good about giving
- *Empowering* because people are acknowledged for the value they offer

Once people contribute in any way to your accomplishments, be sure to connect with them periodically to communicate how you have progressed and let them know again how much you appreciate what they have contributed. You strengthen your network as you share your accomplishments with the people who have assisted you in fulfilling your goals and desired outcomes.

Having Your Grapevine Work for You!

Remember that old familiar, childhood game of gossip? The game begins when one person whispers something to the next person, and then the next person, and so on down the line. What the last person hears is nothing like the original communication. That's okay—and it's even fun when you're playing a game—but not when you desire to have your marketing message passed along your personal word-of-mouth grapevine.

Your word-of-mouth "grapevine" can be a valuable and extremely cost-effective marketing tool that helps you accomplish all your goals more quickly and easily. When your marketing message is clear, it can be easily passed along to people who will be responsive to it. Word-of-mouth marketing starts with you; it's about you having a product or service that people are so pleased with that they choose to tell others about it.

Tips for Activating Your Own Word-of-Mouth Grapevine
  1. **Create a memorable, easily repeatable brand statement.**

      Make it easy for people to talk about you by giving them the words to say. Create a powerful brand with a tagline or slogan that is easy for people to remember and repeat. Communicate your brand statement as often as possible via your business card, online profiles, brochure, press kit, and website. Make sure your brand clearly communicates the image and message you choose to have people think of when they think of you—so that they will pass along your "message" accurately when they tell other people about you.

2. **Provide quality service and treat people with respect.**
   Make sure respect is present in everything you do and say. Respect creates a feeling of honor, which nourishes people at a soul level. Communicate your commitment to "respect" by the way that you speak. Assurance let's a person relax because they know that they can trust what you say. For example:
   - "We *respect* the importance of making sure your participants are ..."
   - "We *respect* your need to have a program that ..."
   - "We *assure* you that any speaker we recommend ..."

3. **Connecting Via Your Introduction**
   Think about how often you have an opportunity to introduce yourself to people either one-on-one, in a group, face-to-face, or online. Your introduction can set the tone for either creating a connection or not. You are more likely to connect with people when you introduce yourself in a way that is clear and concise, both personable and professional, and flows easily and naturally. Most people introduce themselves by merely giving their name, title, and the name of their company. To more easily connect with people, include in your introduction a phrase or tag line that helps people relate to what you can do for them.

   If you grew up hearing the phrase, "Don't toot your own horn!" and responded by not wanting to talk about yourself at all, then now is the time to learn to speak up. Speak with pride and confidence about who you are and what you offer. Give people enough information so they know how to have a conversation with you and also, so they will know how to pass your information along to others. You don't have to brag or be aggressive; instead speak with pride and confidence about who you are and what you have to offer.

Ways to respond to the question, "What do you do?"
- "I make sure my clients …."
- "I enjoy …."
- "I am committed to working with people to …."
- "I am dedicated to …."
- "I love working with …. to …."
- "My focus is to …."
- "I love helping people …."

4. **Ask people to spread the word.**

   Ask people to help you reach others who can benefit from the services you provide. With a little encouragement, people will refer you and pass along your information to others. Networking is a powerful way to create more visibility for yourself and generate new business. People can easily pass along your information by reposting on a social media site, by commenting on one of your posts, and by sending online introductions.

5. **Give people something great to talk about.**

   Be creative and do something extraordinary that gets people's attention. What can you do that will just naturally get people talking? It could be a community project, a new book, a unique program, or sponsoring an industry-related event. Get your customers/clients involved in what you're doing and post information on your social media sites regarding what you're doing that's unique, fun, and interesting. When your clients and customers are part of the excitement they just naturally tell others.

6. **Stay in touch with people.**

   When you stay in touch with people, they are more likely to think of you when they have that perfect opportunity to recommend you to others. Keep your communication lines open so that you stay in conversation with the people in your network. It is through those interactions and conversations that ideas and opportunities get created. There are plenty of reasons for being in touch with people. Follow your inspiration and reach out to contact someone:

- When a specific name pops into your head.
- When you read an article that reminds you of someone's topic, hobby, or profession.
- When you happen to meet a person that knows someone you already know.
- When you think of an opportunity that could be of value to someone.
- When you think of someone who could be of help to you.

After connecting with someone new, whether in person or online, take a moment to send a personal note by mail, email, or via an online social media site. Your note might be a thank you, a "nice to meet you, here's some information that might be of interest to you," "I look forward to seeing you at next month's meeting," or it may include a link to an interesting article that pertains to that person's business. (Check out www. NetworkingWithKindness.com for a list of online resources for creating and mailing customized cards.) Once you meet someone face-to-face, go online and connect with them via your social media sites. Stay in touch with people with a blend of online and offline activities.

Oh yeah, and stay in touch simply to stay in touch. Rather than always calling to sell, prospect, or ask for something, occasionally call friends, clients, and associates for no other reason than to say "hi." This type of "staying in touch" call can be the most meaningful of all in keeping your relationships strong.

People Talk!

Remember, people talk! They talk about everything from their accomplishments and joys to their frustrations and disappointments. People tend to talk more about their disappointments as a way to vent their frustration. In fact, statistics indicate that every unsatisfied client tells at least eight people about their dissatisfaction and unpleasant experience. The "multiplier effect" would kick in when the original eight told another eight, and so on. But with today's social media, a "negative message" can spread from one person to thousands with just the click of a mouse.

But what if, instead, people are spreading a positive message. What if your customers are so pleased with their experience with you and your business that they tell eight people, who then tell another eight, and so on? And what if one of them uses social media to put out the good word? The results can be huge as a message goes viral based on one person's opinion or comment.

Everyone has a vast and potentially powerful network. And your network can be your word-of-mouth market grapevine if you keep the links strong and conversations alive. If your connections have become weak and rusty from neglect, clean up those communication lines so that your grapevine becomes a source of support for your goals to be fulfilled. Networking, relationship marketing, and word-of-mouth marketing are instrumental in people talking to others about you in a way that brings you more business and more contacts.

People need to know who you are, what you do, and the benefits associated with working with you. It is up to you to initiate a word-of-mouth grapevine that creates positive visibility. Creating this type of visibility is critical—it is the way that the people who are looking for what you offer can find you.

Networking for a Greater Good

Networking is great for accomplishing personal goals and business goals, and yet the possibilities with networking are so much greater than just fulfilling any one person's goals. For me, networking has never been just about getting leads, finding new customers, or growing my business. Instead, it is also about connecting in a way that is spiritually fulfilling, personally satisfying, and mutually rewarding. And I notice that as I help others, I benefit as well, sometimes in surprising ways. Networking for a greater good includes a commitment to not only one's self and one's business; there is also great pleasure and pride in being a source for greater good in the world.

Networking and social action are natural, powerful partners. In the past, people interested in social change had to work very hard to find ways to connect with other individuals and groups with whom they could partner and combine resources to fulfill their visions. The Internet makes it dramatically easier for people to find ways to connect, communicate, and rally for a "cause."

When you make a commitment to be a resource for good in the world, you become more aware of opportunities for yourself and others. Here are some ways to multiply your networking awareness:

- Think about ways to share your network with people who are making a difference. What have you accomplished that has provided you with experience and knowledge that can be of great benefit to a social cause or non-profit organization?

- Identify a cause that is near and dear to your heart and network in some way to support this cause. Follow your heart and give the people in your network a chance to support your passion. Every year I participate in a drumming charity event (Texas Big Beat) and I invite the people in my network to get involved as well by volunteering, participating, or making a donation through my personal fundraising page, http://www.FirstGiving.com/DonnaFisher.

- Stay attuned to the value of connecting with meaningful projects. So many people feel disconnected because they don't extend themselves to others—and this "disconnected" feeling can lead to destructive behaviors. The positive feelings that come from networking—a sense of belonging, feeling valued, being able to contribute—all satisfy basic human desires. Satisfying these basic human desires can make a huge difference in having people make choices to contribute to our society and our world.

- Focus on building a network—not just for you—but because you can be of greater service to others when you have a vast, powerful network. When I have a vast, diverse, strong network, I have more to offer you and there is an even greater chance of creating a greater good in the world.

- Network from your heart. Let your caring nature be expressed and fulfilled by being aware of opportunities to be helpful to the people in your life. Your power comes from your ability to stay aware, in tune, and perceptive to yourself and what's going on in your world. Your network shapes who you are, who you are yet to be, and the world around you!

Connecting with people is connecting with life. Networking is personal because it is about people; it is about people connecting with one another. And it is through connecting with people that we connect with life. Networking is not just a good idea, it is basic to who we are as humans.

BALANCE FOR FULFILLING YOUR GOALS WITH NETWORKING

Brain Gym Balances can be used for any issue or area in your life. However, since this is a book on networking, we're going to focus on your networking skills in the Brain Gym Balances. Simply look at the information that Donna has shared in this chapter and then look at Step 2 in the Balance, Checking Donna's Main Points. If you don't see your issues covered in Step 2, then go to Step 3, Identifying Trigger Points for Yourself, and write down any Trigger Point issues that came up for you and then in the column Positive Goal Statements re-write it as a positive statement.

The Balance for Fulfilling Your Goals with Networking is designed to reorganize the energy in your brain and body so you can network more effectively. After doing this Balance, a person who didn't previously utilize networking effectively will now have the capability of doing so if he chooses to. This ability to choose will have been anchored into the brain and body.

STEP 1. CALIBRATION: Preparation for Balancing Process

If necessary, refer to the more detailed instructions on Calibration on page 71.

1. **Water and Hydration:** To make sure you are well hydrated, drink some water.
2. **Electrical Circuitry:** To make sure your electrical circuitry is operating efficiently, do Brain Buttons (page 61).
3. **Activating:** To make sure your body is ready to move, do The Cross Crawl (page 65).
4. **Stress Reduction:** To make sure your stress response is deactivated, do Hook-ups (page 63).
5. **Method to Use:** Select whether you will do Muscle Checking with a Partner, Self Muscle Checking, or Noticing (pages 39 to 54). (View online muscle checking demonstrations at www.SwitchedOnNetworking.com/demo.)
6. **"Yes"/"No" Response:** Use the biofeedback response method you chose to ask your body for a "yes" and then a "no" response (page 45).

NOTE: When you are in the middle of a Balance, it's possible you may begin to get inaccurate or questionable results. While this rarely occurs, it is a possibility. In case it does occur, simply repeat the Calibration procedure, and then proceed with the Balance, beginning at the point where you began to experience the inaccurate or questionable results.

STEP 2. CHECKING DONNA'S MAIN POINTS:

Make the following statements one at a time and do Muscle Checking with a Partner, Self Muscle Checking, or Noticing to determine if your body is switched-on or off after saying each statement. If you are Muscle Checking with a Partner, read it out loud. Place a check mark next to any statements for which you are switched-off.

_____ 1. "I am willing to have the people in my network support me in easily reaching my goals."

_____ 2. "I consistently and confidently make requests for support in accomplishing my goals in all areas of my life."

_____ 3. "I maintain my confidence and carry on with my networking no matter how people respond to me."

_____ 4. "When I make requests of others, I do so in a way that empowers, inspires, and acknowledges them."

_____ 5. "I feel confident developing a network of people that I can call on and count on."

_____ 6. "I use my networking skills for both philanthropic and business purposes."

_____ 7. "I am comfortable calling on my network as a resource for causes and goals that are meaningful to me."

If you were switched-on for all of these statements that means you don't have any major issues with this aspect of the networking process. If this is the case, then go to the next Step to make sure that you don't have any Trigger Points.

STEP 3. IDENTIFYING TRIGGER POINTS FOR YOURSELF:

As we discussed previously, we're now going to give you the opportunity to identify any other Trigger Points that came up for you in this chapter and write them down. Does anything that you've just read act as a Trigger Point for you that's not covered in Step 2, Checking Donna's Main Points?

If you do have a problem or challenge with something that you just read, then on the left side of the column below, briefly write the aspect(s) of Donna's information that is triggering you and switching you off. On the right side of the column, write a goal statement about that Trigger Point in a positive statement, as if you have already easily and effortlessly accomplished it. Even though the Trigger Point may have some negative feelings or thoughts attached to it, or the situation currently feels like a problem or challenge, it's important to write the goal statement with positive language because this represents the new wiring you are creating in your brain. This is what the Brain Gym movements will assist you in switching on.

If more than one Trigger Point comes up, write all of them down in the left column. If there's not enough room below, use another piece of paper. After you have written all your Trigger Points, again write a positive goal statement for each Trigger Point.

If you don't have any Trigger Points come up for you in this section, that simply means that either you're comfortable with the information in this chapter or that your issue or issues were covered in the Major Aspect statements. In that case, go to Step 5 and do the Brain Gym movements and exercises to move yourself to an even higher level of networking success.

TRIGGER POINTS **POSITIVE GOAL STATEMENTS**

_____ _____

_____ _____

_____ _____

_____ _____

_____ _____

_____ _____

_____ _____

_____ _____

_____ _____

If you did write down any additional Trigger Point statements from Donna's material, do Muscle Checking with a Partner, Self Muscle Check, or Noticing on both the negative goal side and the positive goal side of what you wrote. If you are Muscle Checking with a Partner, read the statements out loud and then muscle check each one. You should be switched-off for the statements in both columns. If you are not switched-off, then what you thought was a negative Trigger Point is not one.

NOTE: When you are in the middle of a Balance, it's possible you may begin to get inaccurate or questionable results. While this rarely occurs, it is a possibility. In case it does occur, simply repeat the Calibration procedure, and then proceed with the Balance, beginning at the point where you began to experience the inaccurate or questionable results.

STEP 4. PUTTING YOUR STATEMENTS INTO ACTION

Now do a physical action, role play, or visualization for each of the Major Aspects you checked as switching you off. Next do it for the Trigger Points that you were switched-off for. Do each action for twenty seconds or so and then do Muscle Checking with a Partner, Self Muscle Checking, or Noticing as soon as you complete each action. Place a check mark next to each action for which you are switched-off.

Purpose of Doing Actions: Let me explain the purpose of this step. You should do actions only for the statements above that caused you to be switched-off. This part of the Balance allows you to check your response to the physical impact of attempting to do the various elements of the goal-setting process. In this part, you will be discovering if you are switched-off at the level of the body.

It's actually possible to be switched-off for a statement in Step 2 and 3, but be switched-on when you do the action in Step 4. This means your block for this part of goal setting is not in the physical doing of the action; rather, your block is solely in your mind. For example, after you read the statement, "My goals are easily reached *through the generous support of the people in my network," you might be switched-off when you do Muscle Checking with a Partner, Self Muscle Checking, or Noticing, and when you do an action related to "My goals are easily reached through the generous support of the people in my network" you might be switched-on.*

After you do the Brain Gym movements and exercises in this Balance, the final outcome will be that you will be switched-on for all of the statements, as well as any actions for which you had been switched-off.

STEP 5. CHOOSING TO INCLUDE THE PAST:

Say to yourself (or out loud to your partner, if you are working with a partner):

"My system now incorporates, in the most appropriate way, all relevant past events, known and unknown, into the Step 2, 3 and 4 experience." (See page 45 for explanation for what "yes" or "no" means). Now do Muscle Checking with a Partner, Self Muscle Checking, or Noticing.

STEP 6. REWIRING: Doing the Brain Gym Movements

Now is the time to do the Brain Gym movements listed below:

- The Cross Crawl (see page 65)
- Brain Buttons (see page 61)
- The Thinking Cap (see page 69)
- Lazy 8s (see page 63)
- Hook-ups (see page 63)
- The Positive Points (see page 69)
- Belly Breathing (see page 60)
- Alphabet 8s (see page 59)
- Balance Buttons (see page 60)

STEP 7. CHECKING DONNA'S MAIN POINTS AND YOUR TRIGGER POINTS

Now you're going to recheck the statements from Steps 2 and 3 to make sure you are switched-on for all of the Statements. If you are doing Muscle Checking with a Partner read the statements out loud, or do Self Muscle Checking, or Noticing.

1. "I am willing to have the people in my network support me in easily reaching my goals."
2. "I consistently and confidently make requests for support in accomplishing my goals in all areas of my life."
3. "I maintain my confidence and carry on with my networking no matter how people respond to me."
4. "When I make requests of others, I do so in a way that empowers, inspires, and acknowledges them."
5. "I feel confident developing a network of people that I can call on and count on."
6. "I use my networking skills for both philanthropic and business purposes."
7. "I am comfortable calling on my network as a resource for causes and goals that are meaningful to me."

Repeat the Actions that you did in Step 4, doing each of them for at least twenty seconds. This time when you do the action, you will find that you are switched-on for it. It will be easier to do and you will be able to do it with less stress.

STEP 8. WHERE ARE YOU NOW?

Now that you've completed the Balance for Fulfilling Your Goals with Networking, it's time to reassess your level of improvement or change from your responses to the questionnaire on page 96. You'll find the statements that relates to this particular Balance below.

Place a check mark in the column that most clearly reflects your level of agreement or disagreement with the statement below. Then compare your initial response to your current response. Additionally, I urge you to mark your calendar and re-check your response a month from now to assess your continued improvement. Many people find that their improvement level has even increased even more a month later.

		Strongly Disagree	Disagree	Doesn't Apply	Agree	Strongly Agree
1.	I accomplish my networking goals easily and effectively.					
2.	I feel confident and strong in making clear requests that support my personal and professional goals.					

STEP 9. IT'S TIME TO CELEBRATE

If you're Self Muscle Checking or Noticing, congratulate yourself. If you're working with a partner, celebrate the successful completion of the Balance for Fulfilling Your Goals with Networking and switching yourself on.

Enjoy your new state and your success in applying Donna's information on fulfilling your goals with networking.

STEP 10. REINFORCING THE BALANCE WITH HOME PLAY

Each time you finish reading and doing the Balances for the day, there's one more step before you end your Switched-On Networking session. Home play gives you the opportunity to reinforce and enhance the re-wiring and rebalancing in the brain if your mind-body feels it would be beneficial to do so. Go to Chapter 14 on page 231 and follow the directions there.

NOTE: If you are continuing to work in this current session, skip this step, and go on to the next chapter. Then, after you complete the last Balance you plan to do for the day, go to Chapter 14 and do the Home Play.

CHAPTER 8

BEING AN EFFECTIVE NETWORKER USING YOUR PEOPLE SKILLS

Identify Statements for Balance Section:

As you read through Donna's section below, be aware of any discomfort or negativity that comes to mind about the specific suggestions she makes. Make note of these responses and, when you get to the balance, if those issues are not covered, you'll have the opportunity to write them down.

Have you ever met someone who does everything "right" when networking? He asks engaging questions, makes eye contact, follows up promptly, and even gives you a lead. And yet you don't truly feel connected. There's no sense of rapport. In fact, despite everything, you're not quite sure if you would be interested in meeting with this person again? How could that be if he did everything "right"? The reason is because networking is very much a "people thing." And having effective people skills involves being with people in such a way that they relate to you, trust you, connect with you, and feel good when they're with you.

If networking were simply about *doing* the right things, then any robot could be programmed to network for you. And someone who is all *doing* and no *being* will likely come across as a "robot," very mechanical, saying everything right—and yet there's something missing. The missing piece is *being*—which gets to the heart of networking.

Networking is a blend of awareness, attitude, skills, and habits. If you approach networking like a technique for getting results, or getting what you want, or impressing people, you are missing the boat.

Networking is not a technique. Yes, like others, I can give you tips to stay organized with your network and effective with your follow through. And you can learn how to improve your communication skills and make requests that people can easily respond to. However, none of this will yield optimum results unless your "practice" of networking involves connecting with people and living a resourceful life.

Networking is really very simple. Treat people with kindness and respect. Be helpful. Be supportive. Be available. Be partners. Share yourself and let others be there for you. It's all in how you "be" with people. How are you being?

Being Aware

Many people network in a haphazard manner. There is no consistency, very little focus, and therefore sporadic results and dissatisfaction. When you're on automatic and going through your day as an unconscious "creature of habit" you are more likely to miss out on clues, signs, and opportunities for connecting and creating. But what a difference it makes when you are aware of the people all around you, focused in each conversation and consistently connecting with the people you meet. Then rather than sporadic results and dissatisfaction, you consistently produce magical results and the satisfaction that comes along with that.

Awareness is an essential part of a conscious, thriving network of opportunities. When you are aware, you are conscious of the people, conversations, and opportunities all around you.

Dr. John Demartini, author of *Inspired Destiny,* talks about how your values guide your life and influence your awareness. Someone who values children will notice anything to do with children when she is at the mall, reading the paper, or surfing the internet. Someone who values entrepreneurship will notice opportunities for business when she is at the mall, reading the paper or surfing the internet. Whatever you value is where your mental radar is calibrated.

When you switch on your networking, your radar will be calibrated to automatically and consistently be aware of people, opportunities, and resources.

As your awareness expands, your consciousness expands, your network expands, and your world expands.
Consider the possibility that opportunities are all around you. But when you are not aware of them, it's as if they don't exist. Your awareness determines your reality and your experience. As your awareness expands, your network—and your opportunities—expand!

In my book, *Professional Networking for Dummies,* I use the example of someone desiring to go to college who doesn't have the funds. There are scholarships available, and yet he doesn't apply, because he's not even aware that there are scholarships. Even though the scholarship money is there, if he's not aware of it, it doesn't do him any good. And he could spend most of his life thinking, "If only I had the money for college, I could have really made something of my life."

It is through networking that you *become aware* of valuable information and opportunities. Then once you become aware you can turn the opportunity into a new reality. Your networking effectiveness expands exponentially when you increase your consciousness. How much consciousness do you bring to your interactions?

Turn Up Your Awareness
To develop your own sense of self and your networking effectiveness, be aware of:
- The network that you already have.
- Your own power and ability as a networker.
- People's natural desire to give and contribute.
- Your value and the value of what you have to give.
- How you can be a resource for the people in your life.
- How your strengths, skills, information, contacts, and expertise can be of value to others.
- What you can offer to the people in your network that will help them accomplish their goals.
- The vast and unlimited nature of your network.
- The way you relate to yourself and the people in your life.

- What people are saying that tells you how you can be a resource for them.
- What you are saying and how you are either creating connection or distance.
- What you are thinking and not saying that—if you were saying it—would generate opportunities.
- The power and opportunity that your network provides to you.
- The willingness and desire of others to contribute to you.
- How networking can be an easy, natural part of your life.
- How networking is an accepted and expected way of relating and doing business.
- That the support and resources you desire is available and right around you—it's yours for the asking!

Being Thoughtful

People tend to think of being thoughtful as being kind or considerate. And that makes sense, although, I think of thoughtful as being "full of thought." When we are full of thought we are more likely to make considerate and productive choices. Conversely, when we react without thinking, our interactions and behaviors do not always create the most effective results.

Being thoughtful when networking means giving full thought to the ways you can be of support to others and/or what information you can provide to them. Without giving full thought to a situation, the tendency is to think, *"Oh, I don't know anyone to refer them to"* or *"I can't be of any help to them."* Short-sighted thinking stops the thought process before you reach the ideas and opportunities that can be useful to you and someone else.

Being Present

Can you recall a time you were talking with someone and it was obvious their thoughts and attention were somewhere other than with you? When you're interacting with someone who is not really *present*, it's pretty noticeable. If their thoughts and attention are somewhere else, then they are not really being with you. There is no way to connect with someone when they are not present! It seems pretty obvious when you think about it, right?

However, when someone is fully present, you are more likely to become fully engaged and connect with her. You can remember the interaction and recall it easily. An interaction with a person who is fully present is likely to establish a strong link in your network because you automatically connect with that person on a deeper level.

It can be easy to meet a lot of people. And yet what's important is whether you are connecting with the people you meet. "Being present" with someone can turn a chance meeting into a quality connection. People often talk about their desire for more quality time with their children, spouse, and friends. "Quality time" is created by your attention to the people you are with whether that's family, friends or business associates.

In today's world, being present is more challenging than ever. Technology vies for everyone's attention 24/7. However, being present with someone is the greatest acknowledgement you can give them as being a worthy and valued individual.

So the question is, how can you be present and, even more so, how can you stay present? Being present—and staying present—comes from your commitment to people and your ability to focus. When you are present you are focused on the moment rather than letting your thoughts and attention float off elsewhere. As you develop your natural ability to listen, interact, and connect with people wherever you are, your networking will consist of more and more quality interactions - quality time. In the process, you will be building a quality network that can support and enrich your life personally and professionally.

Being Gracious

There's a poem titled "Anyway" by Kent Keith which includes the following:

The good you do today will be forgotten tomorrow.
Do good anyway.
Honesty and frankness will make you vulnerable.
Be honest and frank anyway.

This poem comes to mind when I think about being gracious as a networker. There may be times when people forget your name, don't follow up like they said they would, or rush off to go talk to someone else. Be gracious anyway!

At networking events, you've possibly experienced the opposite of graciousness. You may have felt the sting of being abruptly "dismissed" when the person you were talking with made a determination that you were not a candidate for their product or service and abruptly scurried away to find a "candidate." Their rude end to the conversation may have been upsetting and frustrating. But we can't let others impact how we deal with the world or our own sensibilities regarding networking. If we did so, we could easily miss out on a connection with the next person who comes along—and that person might be the one who will present us with a golden opportunity.

The word gracious means "courteous, elegant, with ease." Being gracious calls on you to have the strength to treat people with respect and dignity because that's who you are. Being gracious is, after all, a choice you make. You choose to be gracious rather than be influenced by others who choose otherwise.

In relationship to networking, you are being gracious when you acknowledge the presence of people around you, treat people with respect, invite someone into a group conversation, include people at a dinner table or invite them to join an activity, and value them for who they are. Gracious people are appreciative of the contributions of others and also respectful of their time and talents.

Being Open-Minded and Broad-Minded

A closed or judgmental mind blocks opportunities. If you say something is impossible, then it is likely that you will prove yourself to be right. If you are open to something being possible even when it seems impossible, you are ripe for creating new and exciting opportunities for yourself.

Be mentally receptive to new information and ideas. Rigid thinking restricts your view. If you are not open and receptive, you will miss out on information that is available and right around you. If you have a tendency to think you already know everything and/or want to be the one who has all the answers, then there is very little room for new information to get to you. It's the old analogy of attempting to pour liquid into a glass that is already full. The liquid then runs over and out. Once the glass is emptied and there is room for more, then the liquid can be added.

To keep an open-mind, discipline yourself to think "what if?" By inquiring—rather than deciding—your mind begins to think beyond automatic thinking into creative thinking.

1. *"What if* someone in my network could help me connect with… !"
2. *"What if* I already have connections in my new industry and I just don't realize it yet!"
3. *"What if… !"*

Being Empowering

It's easy to empower others—and it rarely takes much effort. Empower means "to give power or authority." When you focus on giving positive energy to others, people are generally so appreciative that you get so much more back than you give.

Sometimes all it takes to empower someone is to show an interest in who they are and what they're doing. When you acknowledge, encourage, support other people, you are empowering them to believe in themselves, take positive action, and move forward with whatever they are creating as positive results in their lives.

And here's the real bonus—when you empower others, you are automatically empowering yourself at the same time.

Being Dimensional

It is so easy to "peg" people and label them by their brand, their profession, where they live, their hobbies, the types of clothes they wear, the car they drive, the types of food they eat, etc. We don't label people to be judgmental or negative; it happens on the subconscious level and we usually don't even realize that we're doing it.

When we "peg" people according to specific labels, we unconsciously stop learning about other aspects of them. That's not positive for networking opportunities because once you make a decision about someone, you are limiting them and you are therefore also limiting yourself. In essence, you are killing off other options. (Did you know that the word decision actually means to "cut off" or "kill off"? Think about homicide, suicide, and pesticides.)

Even the people you *think* you already know might have resources you don't know about that would greatly enhance your profession, your hobbies, and/or your lifestyle. When we are open to seeing ourselves and others as multi-dimensional, we are more likely to learn more about people than just what's obvious.

Who you are consists of all of your job/career experiences, life experiences, and the people who influence you as a person. You are larger than what you see in your mirror; you are a culmination of connections that provide an intricate net of information.

Being Flexible—and Flowing

It's great to have a roadmap, to have a business plan. Planning is great. Planning helps me think through my outcome, resources, actions, and timelines. And, at the same time, there are moments when huge opportunities present themselves only because we are flexible and choose to go with the flow.

Sometimes it's actually better to step beyond any pre-determined plan or preconceived ideas because being too rigid and structured can hinder our receptivity to a better idea that presents itself along the way. I'm sure most of you have experienced situations in which even the greatest plan evolved in a different and much more beneficial direction once we got on board and started executing it.

Some of my most rewarding accomplishments have happened when I had a very clear outcome in mind and yet had no idea how to get there. By taking one step at a time, and using a powerful network of resources, the steps became clear as I progressed.

So stay aware. When you are on task with your plan, it's possible that you will encounter opportunities, suggestions, and people who enhance your plan in ways you could never even imagine. After all, that's why we network and that's why we stay flexible.

Being of Service

Networking truly is about serving others to achieve their highest good. It is about being a resource so that others live true to their dreams, their potential, and their purpose in life. Just imagine—when everyone is committed to having everyone around them live true to their highest good—what a wonderful world!

Bob Littell came up with the term Power NetWeaving to represent what he refers to as "Do-a-Favr Marketing™." It's based on "Doing favors for people, doing those favors over a long period of time, and asking for nothing in return." But there is one more aspect to Power NetWeaving, and that is that we *trust* that those "favors will pay off, sometimes in a very big way."

Bob relates NetWeaving to customer service. He reminds us that "when people are served and treated well, they come back for more." And the same is true with networking. When people in your network are served by you and treated well by you, "they return again and again," which means your network keeps flowing and growing.

Being Fun

Meeting people and networking with people can be fun! This is true even for those of us who tend to be shy and have introversion tendencies. One of the ways to get beyond the "shyness" is to "lighten up," don't take yourself or others too seriously and get your attention off yourself.

Be lighthearted and slightly playful in your interactions and you will put yourself and others at ease so that the networking can happen more naturally. If you get too serious about the results you desire to produce, you may miss out on the enjoyment and the results. If you take yourself too seriously and are too intense, you may "scare" people away. After all, we all prefer to connect with people that we are comfortable around—and that we can have fun with.

For me, part of the fun of networking is the "not knowing." You never really know who you might meet that will become a great connection for you.

When you're having fun interacting with people, you are more likely to connect in a way that leads to a positive, professional, supportive relationship. So bring a pleasant, playful spirit with you when you're networking and then notice just how easy it can be for conversations to flow.

BALANCE FOR BEING AN EFFECTIVE NETWORKER

This Balance is designed to switch you on for being an effective networker. In this Balance, Step 5, the Taking Action Step uses the Dennison Laterality Repatterning (DLR). Let me give you some history of the DLR. Years ago researchers Dolman and Delacatto found that when children with learning disabilities did The Cross Crawl along the floor, their grades improved in school. (See The Cross Crawl on page 65.) However, when this work started to spread into school systems, teachers reported mixed results. It worked with some of the children but not with others. It turns out that some children were actually switched-off for The Cross Crawl. In other words, The Cross Crawl had a positive effect for some children but not for others. Those who were not switched-on for The Cross Crawl were operating homolaterally, meaning that only one side of the brain was operating at a time, instead of both sides. Research by Dr. Paul Dennison indicated that this homolateral brain functioning contributed to their learning disabilities.

Again, it was Dr. Dennison's work that created a breakthrough when he developed the method that became known as Dennison Laterality Repatterning (DLR). After doing DLR, those who were previously switched-off for The Cross Crawl were now switched-on, which meant the positive benefits of The Cross Crawl became accessible to everyone.

A research study that measured motor coordination skills in students showed the positive impact of hemisphere integration using DLR used in the Brain Gym process. In this study the students were divided into three groups. The control group did nothing and, at the end of the study, their motor coordination skills were unchanged. The second group of students did a series of Brain Gym movements and exercises for five minutes each day. At the end of the study, this group showed a statistically significant improvement in their motor coordination abilities. The third group did DLR just once, at the very beginning of the study, and then every day they did the same Brain Gym movements and exercises as the second group. The only thing different between these two groups was that one group had done DLR one time. At the end of the study, the group that did the DLR had a rate of improvement more than double that of the second group, indicating that DLR has a profound impact on brain integration. (This study is available at www.Teplitz.com/BrainGymResearch.)

Why is DLR so helpful? Let's use the analogy of high gear and low gear responses from the body. An example of a high gear response is when you're driving your car on the interstate. If traffic is light, driving doesn't take a lot of effort or energy, and you make really good time. It's so easy, and you can cover a great distance in a shorter time frame. That's the high gear concept. An example of low gear is when you come to an accident or a lane closure due to road construction as you are driving. It's a new and unfamiliar situation. You have to slow down to figure out what to do next. This situation requires a homolateral response, with each hemisphere of the brain firing independently of the other as you navigate this new situation.

The ideal is to have both hemispheres of the brain firing and communicating easily and effectively depending on the situation. For example, when you pass by the construction situation on the highway, you easily move right back into high gear and, once again, you are cruising along. This is what is called integrated high and low gear.

What I'm looking for you to achieve is to have your body automatically function from the highest state of integration. This will allow you to easily stop and clearly think when you're in a new networking situation, as well as access your natural networking skills.

This integrated state allows you to move quickly and efficiently from the whole picture to the individual parts of the networking process—without getting stuck in one or the other.

When you are cruising along as a successful and effective networker, you are in integrated high gear, which feels natural, effortless, and easy since it is based on a process you have learned well. Then, when you encounter a new networking situation, you will be able to momentarily pause, think, and creatively meet this new challenge. The ability to do this is called integrated low gear. When you come to a new networking situation, integrated low gear allows you to gear down at the appropriate moment. Then, as soon as you've mastered the new situation, you are able to easily and effortlessly switch back to being in high gear.

The Balance that follows will allow you to experience the impact of Dennison Laterality Repatterning so you can experience the change at a very deep level in terms of the networking process. Your feelings and attitudes about networking will be enhanced and uplifted. In addition, by switching you on for The Cross Crawl, you will also be switching yourself on for all of the Brain Gym movements and exercises. This means that any of these movements and exercises that you do in the other Balances will have an even more positive impact on you.

STEP 1. CALIBRATION: Preparing for the Process

If necessary, refer to the more detailed instructions on Calibration on page 71.

1. **Water and Hydration:** To make sure you are well hydrated, drink some water.

2. **Electrical Circuitry:** To make sure your electrical circuitry is operating efficiently, do Brain Buttons (page 61).

3. **Activating:** To make sure your body is ready to move, do The Cross Crawl (page 65).

4. **Stress Reduction:** To make sure your stress response is deactivated, do Hook-ups (page 63).

5. **Method to Use:** Select whether you will do Muscle Checking with a Partner, Self Muscle Checking, or Noticing (pages 39-54). (View online muscle checking demonstrations at www.SwitchedOnNetworking.com/demo.)

6. **"Yes"/"No" Response:** Use the biofeedback response method you chose to ask your body for a "yes" and then a "no" response (page 45).

NOTE: When you are in the middle of a Balance, it's possible you may begin to get inaccurate or questionable results. While this rarely occurs, it is a possibility. In case it does occur, simply repeat the Calibration procedure, and then proceed with the Balance beginning at the point where you began to experience the inaccurate or questionable results.

STEP 2: CHECKING DONNA'S MAIN POINTS

Read the following statements one at a time and do Muscle Checking with a Partner, Self Muscle Checking, or Noticing to determine if your body is switched-on or switched-off after saying each statement. If you are Muscle Checking with a Partner, read each statement out loud. Place a check mark next to any statements for which you are switched-off:

_____ 1. "I easily switch from 'doing mode' to 'being mode' in order to be present with people."

_____ 2. "I am open and receptive to the opportunities available to me through the people in my network."

_____ 3. "I am flexible and willing to incorporate new ideas."

_____ 4. "I love being of service to help people achieve their highest good."

_____ 5. "I know that I have value to offer to the people in my network."

_____ 6. "I have fun interacting with people and exploring opportunities."

STEP 3. IDENTIFYING TRIGGER POINTS FOR YOURSELF:

In the chart below, write down any statements from Donna's material (that aren't already listed above), that triggered an uncomfortable or negative response for you. In the right-hand column, write out your positive goal regarding the Trigger Point you identified. Muscle Check with a Partner, Self Muscle Check or Notice on both the negative side (Trigger Point) and the positive goal side of what you wrote. If you are Muscle Checking with a Partner, read the statements out loud. If you are switched off, then place a check mark by that Trigger Point. If you find that you are switched-on for the Trigger Point and positive goal statement, then what you thought was a negative Trigger Point is not one.

TRIGGER POINTS	POSITIVE GOAL STATEMENTS

If you are switched-on for all of Donna's Main Points and you did not identify any Trigger Points for yourself, then you don't have any major issues or difficulties with the information in this chapter. If this is the case, skip to Step 6 and do the DLR. By doing the DLR, you will be switching yourself on so all of the Brain Gym movements and exercises will have an even more positive impact on you.

STEP 4. ACTIONS

Now do a physical activity, role play, or visualization for at least twenty seconds for each of Donna's Main Points and for the Trigger Points you were switched-off for in Steps 2 and 3. Do Muscle Checking with a Partner, Self Muscle Checking, or Noticing for the actions as soon as you complete each one and place a check mark next to each action for which you are switched-off.

STEP 5. CHOOSING TO INCLUDE THE PAST:

Say to yourself (or out loud to your partner, if you are working with a partner): "My system now incorporates, in the most appropriate way, all relevant past events, known and unknown, into my experience." Now do Muscle Checking with a Partner, Self Muscle Checking, or Noticing for a "yes" or "no" response. (See page 45 for an explanation of a "yes" or "no" response.)

STEP 6. TAKING ACTION: Dennison Laterality Repatterning

Turn to page 143 to do the Dennison Laterality Repatterning (DLR). Once you finish the Dennison Laterality Repatterning, go on to Step 7 below.

STEP 7. CHECKING DONNA'S MAIN POINTS AND YOUR TRIGGER POINTS AFTER DOING THE DLR

Now you're going to recheck the statements from Steps 2 and 3 to make sure you are switched-on for all of the Statements. If you are doing Muscle Checking with a Partner read the statements out loud, or do Self Muscle Checking, or Noticing.
1. "I easily switch from 'doing mode' to 'being mode' in order to be present with people."
2. "I am open and receptive to the opportunities available to me through the people in my network."
3. "I am flexible and willing to incorporate new ideas."
4. "I love being of service to help people achieve their highest good."

5. "I know that I have value to offer to the people in my network."

6. "I have fun interacting with people and exploring opportunities."

Repeat the Actions that you did in Step 4, doing each of them for at least twenty seconds. This time when you do the action, you will find that you are switched-on for it. It will be easier to do and you will be able to do it with less stress.

STEP 8. WHERE ARE YOU NOW?

Now that you've completed the Balance for Being an Effective Networker, it's time to reassess your level of improvement or change from your responses to the questionnaire on page 96. You'll find the questions that relate to this particular Balance below.

Place a check mark in the column that most clearly reflects your level of agreement or disagreement with each statement below. Then compare your initial response to your current response. Additionally, I urge you to mark your calendar and re-check your responses a month from now to assess your continued improvement. Many people find that their improvement level has increased even more a month later.

		Strongly Disagree	Disagree	Doesn't Apply	Agree	Strongly Agree
3.	I am an effective networker.					
4.	I enjoy networking and being a resource for people.					
5.	I easily connect with people and build strong relationships.					
6.	I am inspired to be of service to others.					

STEP 9. IT'S TIME TO CELEBRATE

If you're Self Muscle Checking or Noticing, congratulate yourself. If you're working with a partner, celebrate the successful completion of the Balance for Being an Effective Networker.

STEP 10. REINFORCING THE BALANCE WITH HOME PLAY

Each time you finish reading and doing the Balances for the day, there's one more step before you end your Switched-On Networking session. Home play gives you the opportunity to reinforce and enhance the re-wiring and rebalancing in the brain if your mind-body feels it would be beneficial to do so. Go to Chapter 14 on page 231 and follow the directions there.

NOTE: If you are continuing to work in this current session, skip this step and go on to the next chapter. Then turn to Reinforcing with Home Play after the last Balance you are going to do that day.

DENNISON LATERALITY REPATTERNING

Dennison Laterality Repatterning integrates the left and right sides of the body and brain.

STEP 1. PRE-ACTIVITIES:

Do each activity and do Muscle Checking with a Partner, Self Muscle Checking, or Noticing. Note whether you are switched-on or off for each activity and mark each result in the right-hand column. After you do the Pre-Activities, I'll tell you what the responses should be. If you're not having these responses, don't be concerned, as that's what doing the DLR will change.

• **The Cross Crawl** (see Illustration page 65). Do a half dozen of The Cross Crawls. Then do Muscle Checking with a Partner, Self Muscle Checking, or Noticing to learn whether you are switched-on or off. Mark your response for each part of Step 1 in the column to the right.	Switched: On___ Off___ 
• **Homolateral Crawl** As if you are a puppet on a string, raise the right arm and the right leg up at the same time. Then, after lowering the right arm and leg, raise the left arm and leg up at the same time. Repeat six times. Then do Muscle Checking with a Partner, Self Muscle Checking, or Noticing to learn whether you are switched-on or switched off. Mark your response.	Switched: On___ Off___ 
• **Close your eyes and visualize the letter "X."** Do Muscle Checking with a Partner, Self Muscle Checking, or while you continue to visualize the "X" to learn whether you are switched-on or off and mark your response.	Switched: On___ Off___ 
• **Close your eyes and visualize two parallel lines.** You can think of railroad tracks. Do Muscle Checking with a Partner, Self Muscle Checking, or Noticing while you continue to visualize the parallel lines to learn whether you are switched-on or off. Mark your response.	Switched: On___ Off___ 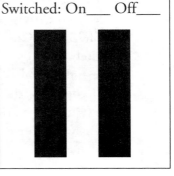

The results you are looking for are:
- Switched-on for The Cross Crawl
- Switched-off for the Homolateral Crawl
- Switched-on for the X
- Switched-off for the parallel lines

As I said before, if your results are a different pattern of "on" and "off," don't be concerned because that's what we are going to change by the end of the Dennison Laterality Repatterning. This means at the end of this Balance, your results will be appropriate.

STEP 2. STARTING THE PROCESS

In starting the Dennison Laterality Repatterning process, you will be doing The Cross Crawl while looking diagonally up to the left and right with just your eyes. You will also be humming a steady note while you first look diagonally up in each direction. The humming is done as a part of this process because we want to keep your logical mind, your left hemisphere, from getting involved in the process. By humming a steady note while doing The Cross Crawl, you are activating the right hemisphere of your brain.

Let's do it now:

Repatterning

1. Do fifteen to twenty of The Cross Crawls while looking diagonally up to the left, keeping your nose facing forward and, at the same time, humming a steady note. Next do fifteen to twenty of The Cross Crawls while looking diagonally up to the right, keeping your nose facing forward and again, at the same time, humming a steady note. Remember to keep your nose pointed straight ahead so only your eyes are looking diagonally up. Do the movements slowly.

2. You are now ready to do the Homolateral Crawl. You will be counting out loud for fifteen to twenty complete repetitions while keeping your nose facing forward. (A complete repetition is raising the arm and leg of one side up

and down and then the other side up and down.) This time you will be looking diagonally down with just your eyes. First look diagonally down to the right for fifteen to twenty repetitions and then repeat the Homolateral Crawl fifteen to twenty more times while looking diagonally down to the left and counting out loud. Do the movements slowly.

STEP 3. INTEGRATION METAPHOR

Hold your arms out to each side as if you are showing someone that you caught a really big fish. Close your eyes and visualize holding the left hemisphere of your brain in your left hand and the right hemisphere of your brain in your right hand. Once you have both hemispheres clearly visualized, begin to physically bring your hands together slowly while you continue to visualize your hemispheres coming together. When your hands meet, intertwine or interlace your fingers. Finally, move your hands to your chest and put a slight pressure on your palms while you feel both sides of your brain coming together. Hold this position for ten or fifteen seconds or longer if you want to. When you are done, release your hands.

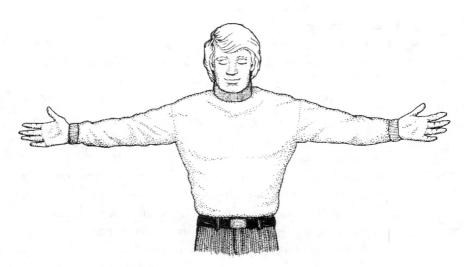

STEP 4. CEMENTING IN THE CROSS CRAWL CHANGES

This part of the process cements in the changes you just made. Keeping your nose facing straight ahead, do The Cross Crawl for approximately thirty seconds, while you are rotating your eyes in circles. First rotate several times in one direction and then rotate them several times in the opposite direction. You don't have to count the exact number of times. (And, no, you don't hum this time).

STEP 5. CEMENTING IN THE HOMOLATERAL CRAWL CHANGES

Keeping your nose facing straight ahead, do the Homolateral Crawl for approximately thirty seconds, while you are rotating your eyes in a circle. First rotate several times in one direction and then do it several times in the opposite direction. (You don't have to count out loud this time.)

STEP 6. POST ACTIVITIES

You are now going to repeat each of the Pre-Activities that you did in Step 1. Do each action and then do Muscle Checking with a Partner, Self Muscle Checking, or Noticing after doing each of the following:

- Do six Cross Crawls. Do Muscle Checking with a Partner, Self Muscle Checking, or Noticing and you should be switched-on.
- Do six Homolateral Crawls. Do Muscle Checking with a Partner, Self Muscle Checking, or Noticing and you should be switched-off.
- Visualize the letter "X." Do Muscle Checking with a Partner, Self Muscle Checking, or Noticing and you should be switched-on.
- Visualize two parallel lines. Do Muscle Checking with a Partner, Self Muscle Checking, or Noticing and you should be switched-off.

The DLR has integrated the left and right sides of your body and brain, resulting in the appropriate responses to these activities. You are now switched-on to be able to naturally experience the Integrated High Gear state while you also have access to the Integrated Low Gear ability to momentarily pause and think clearly in new situations.

STEP 7. FINISHING UP THE DLR
End by doing The Cross Crawl again six more times while visualizing an "X."

STEP 8. Return to Step 7 of the Balance for Being an Effective Networker on page 141 and do the rest of the steps.

CHAPTER 9

NURTURING YOUR NETWORK

Identify Statements for Balance Section:

As you read through Donna's section below, be aware of any discomfort or negativity that comes to mind about the specific suggestions she makes. Make note of these responses and, when you get to the balance, if those issues are not covered, you'll have the opportunity to write them down.

Is your "net" working for you?

- Do you have a network of people that *you know* you can call on—and count on?
- Do people respond to your requests in a positive, helpful manner?
- Are you at ease when meeting new people?
- Do you find it easy to generate interesting conversations?
- Do the people in your network regularly refer you to others who can be valuable resources for you?

If you can confidently answer "yes" to all of these questions, good for you. Your "net" is working well. If not, then your "net" may be stagnant and ready for some fresh energy and direction.

Simply having a network is not the same as having an active, empowering, productive network. Everyone has a network that consists of all the people they know. Your network includes the people you grew up with, went to school with, currently work with or previously worked with, your friends and family, and the people you communicate with and are linked to online. However, having an *active, empowering, productive* network means the people you know are interacting with you and each other, sharing resources, and supporting one another.

Your "net" consists of people linked to you and each other because of common interests, jobs, family, online communities, organizations, and mutual connections. These links create a strong web of connections that can provide a powerful foundation of support. An active network is just naturally growing, shifting, and expanding as we continually meet new people, while also strengthening existing relationships.

You are at the center of your network, and, at the same time, you are a spoke on the networks of all the people you know. Every time you connect with someone new, your network expands and simultaneously so do the networks of everyone you know. And when someone in your network connects with a new person, your network expands as well. Your network is dynamic and ever-evolving.

Nurture Your Network With Appreciation

"Water your tree" by telling people that you appreciate them. Appreciation is a simple and yet powerful way to nurture your relationships which, at the same time, strengthens your network. Have you ever noticed how good it feels when you praise others? Praising people actually creates positive energy. When you acknowledge someone, you are calling attention to something that is positive and helpful that you appreciate about that person. You brighten someone's day while boosting your own attitude of gratitude.

Get in the Habit of Saying Thanks

Sprinkle the word "thanks" throughout your day, letting people know you appreciate them. Be generous with your acknowledgements. As long as you are sincere and your acknowledgement is a gift, you cannot over-acknowledge someone. Be specific and acknowledge people for both what they have done and a quality or characteristic you admire about them. The more specific you are when telling someone what you appreciate about them, the more meaningful the communication will be to them.

Play the Acknowledgment Game

In every conversation this week focus on finding some way to acknowledge the person you are talking with. It could be as simple as, "Thank you for taking the time to visit with me" or "I appreciate hearing your ideas about…" or "You have a great way of expressing your thoughts." Once you play the "Acknowledgement Game" you will find that there are numerous things you can acknowledge others for. Right now, I acknowledge you for reading this book and using Brain Gym to connect with people with greater ease, comfort, and effectiveness.

As you play this game more and more, you will also discover that it's as much fun to acknowledge others as it is to be acknowledged by others. Acknowledge clients, customers, vendors, employees, co-workers, and associates for all that they do to contribute. Thank clients for their trust and the opportunity to do business with them. Thank people for being helpful, easy to work with, responsive to your requests for information, and professional in all their interactions. Let people know what it is that you like and appreciate about working with them, doing business with them, or simply knowing them.

There are many reasons for saying thanks:
- Thanks for the business
- Thanks for the opportunity
- Thanks for your support
- Thanks for the referral
- Thanks for the ideas
- Thanks for the encouragement
- Thanks for the opportunity to learn more about your business
- Thanks for the opportunity to do business with you
- Thanks for taking the time to …"

Here are some ways to play the Acknowledgement Game:
- Send notes/cards
- Send emails
- Say it in person
- Make phone calls

- Tweet about the person
- Post about the person on social media sites

My favorite story about sending notes was shared by a gentleman in one of my workshops. A friend of his had attended his musical performance. Several days later a note came in the mail that said it all in one word—"Stunning!" The man shared how much that simple one-word note meant to him at that time. Even years later, this particular acknowledgement from his friend still stands out for him. It doesn't take much—just one word of acknowledgement expressed sincerely and eloquently can deeply touch another person.

It doesn't have to take much time or effort to communicate your appreciation. In fact, technology has made it easier than ever to play the Acknowledgement Game. Messages of appreciation are frequently posted on social media sites. And it's also easy to use online sites to create cards that can be either emailed or mailed to people. I invite you to join our Networking With Kindness campaign. Go to www.NetworkingWithKindness.com and send a card today to someone you appreciate. Whether you choose to send one note a day or one note a week, the act of consistently expressing acknowledgments and appreciation will ripple through your network. Nurture your network now!

DO THE RIGHT THINGS

The Do's and Don'ts of Effective Networking

If your network is not producing the results you desire, review these tips and upgrade your networking attitudes, actions, and habits. Follow these tips to make sure you are doing the things that enhance, rather than hamper, your networking.

THE DO'S	THE DON'TS
Do initiate conversations.	*Don't* wait for others to approach you.
Do your best to put others at ease.	*Don't* put people on the spot.
Do ask.	*Don't* demand.
Do follow-up.	*Don't* think it's up to the other person to follow up.
Do pass along information.	*Don't* hoard information that can be of value to others.
Do recommend others.	*Don't* guarantee the services of others.
Do call people.	*Don't* get so busy that you lose touch with people.
Do listen.	*Don't* prejudge what you think others have to offer.
Do organize your network.	*Don't* let opportunities fall through the cracks.
Do focus on people.	*Don't* get too focused on yourself.
Do express thanks/appreciation.	*Don't* take your network for granted.
Do speak with pride.	*Don't* downplay the value of what you have to offer.

Keep It Simple Sweetie— The KISS Method of Networking

Networking is as simple as friendship. Through networking you connect with people, build relationships, and share resources. Networking is choosing interdependence over isolation and realizing the power of cooperation over competition—it links people and information to one another for the mutual benefit of everyone involved.

There's really nothing unusual or difficult about networking. Pure and simple, it's about people being friendly, considerate, and helpful. People hang out with people they like. People friend people they like online. People tend to do business with people they like. Your network is working when people are staying connected, being supportive, and sharing information with one another.

Your "net" will grow and produce results when you nurture it—just like watering a fruit tree. When you water a fruit tree, it grows and blossoms and produces fruit. Similarly, a "net" that is fed consistently creates, expands, and produces results. However, going back to our analogy, if you shift your focus to simply picking and eating the fruit and forget to water the tree, at some point, there will be no more fruit and the tree will begin to wither. In the same way it is important that you water your network for it to grow and blossom and consistently produce results.

Nurturing Tips

Unproductive: *Coming across too strong, too quick*
Nurturing: *Give people a chance to warm up to you*
Take little steps in conversation in a safe and non-threatening way to begin to get to know people. Master the art of small talk as a way to connect with people and develop the first stepping stone of relationship. (I'll cover more on this in Chapter 10, Connecting Online and Face-to-Face.)

Unproductive: *Lack of focus*
Nurturing: *Clear intentions*
You can be out there meeting lots of people and yet if you are not focused on giving and receiving support, your efforts could turn into time consuming, unproductive activities. Strengthen your ability to focus – on people, on your goals, on being a resource for others. Your intention for networking to be empowering and rewarding will influence your actions and interactions to produce positive results.

Unproductive: *No follow up*
Nurturing: *Focused follow up*

You can do a great job of meeting people and then miss out on where that could lead if you don't follow up. Oftentimes, follow up doesn't happen because people get busy and get distracted. Get in the habit of staying focused on the people you meet all the way through to the appropriate follow up activities.

Unproductive: *Not paying attention*
Nurturing: *Full attention*

Pay attention! There are opportunities all around you. Simply paying more attention in each conversation will lead to stronger relationships and valuable information. Pay attention to what people are saying, what they're doing, and what they're requesting.

Unproductive: *Meeting people—but not connecting*
Nurturing: *Connecting with the people you meet*

It can be easy to meet a lot of people; however, the important thing is to really connect with the people you meet. You can meet someone, even carry on a conversation with him or her, and not really connect with the person. Connect with people by making eye contact, relating and responding to what they say, and expressing an interest in them. Be curious and interested in people, who they are, and what they have to say.

Unproductive: *Partial listening*
Nurturing: *Fully engaged*

If you are thinking about other things or even doing others things while you are attempting to listen to someone, you will miss out on part of what is being said. And the part that you miss could be a few key words that would have led to a golden networking opportunity. Fine-tune your listening and you will build strong trusting relationships and gather valuable information.

Unproductive: *Monopolizing conversations*
Nurturing: *Generating dialogues*

Get people engaged in conversations with you. If you're monopolizing a conversation, you're not learning anything. Instead of focusing on yourself, get people to talk about themselves so that you can learn more about them. By generating interesting dialogues, people are more likely to feel included and connected and you will discover how you can be of support and what value they have to offer you.

Unproductive: *Inconsistent follow through*
Nurturing: *Follow your promptings*

When you have a thought about calling someone for help or support, make that call! When you think about sending someone a thank you, follow through and send that card! Don't make networking a last resort. Get in the habit of following through on your promptings and networking will happen as just a natural result of being in touch with people. Make networking a priority so that you are always building your network as a strong support system that will be readily accessible to you whenever you have a need.

Unproductive: *Hesitancy to ask for help or support*
Nurturing: *Confidence to ask*

People are often hesitant to ask for help or information for fear of rejection, lack of confidence, or concern about bothering people. And yet, in reality, most people feel flattered, acknowledged, and are glad to help. Reach out with confidence knowing that people tend to have a natural human desire to help, contribute, and be of support. Asking people for help gives them permission to contribute. Anytime you ask someone for help or support you are actually acknowledging them for their value to you and giving them a chance to contribute to you in some way.

Unproductive: *Prejudging*
Nurturing: *Allowing others to choose for themselves*
Anytime you have the thought, "Oh, they won't be able to help me with…" or "They probably don't know anybody who does…" or "They're so busy they wouldn't…" you are prejudging and deciding for other people. Give people the information and opportunity to choose and decide for themselves if and how they can be of service and of value to you and your network.

BALANCE FOR NURTURING
YOUR NETWORKING

In this Balance, you will strengthen your confidence in approaching new contacts, as well as people who are already in your network.

STEP 1. CALIBRATION: Preparing for the Balancing Process
If necessary, refer to the more detailed instructions on Calibration on page 71.
1. **Water and Hydration:** To make sure you are well hydrated, drink some water.
2. **Electrical Circuitry:** To make sure your electrical circuitry is operating efficiently, do Brain Buttons (page 61).
3. **Activating:** To make sure your body is ready to move, do The Cross Crawl (page 65).

4. **Stress Reduction:** To make sure your stress response is deactivated, do Hook-ups (page 63).
5. **Method to Use:** Select whether you will do Muscle Checking with a Partner, Self Muscle Checking, or Noticing (pages 39 to 54). (View online muscle checking demonstrations at www.SwitchedOnNetworking.com/demo.)
6. **"Yes"/"No" Response:** Use the biofeedback response method you chose to ask your body for a "yes" and then a "no" response (page 45).

NOTE: When you are in the middle of a Balance, it's possible you may begin to get inaccurate or questionable results. While this rarely occurs, it is a possibility. In case it does occur, simply repeat the Calibration procedure, and then proceed with the Balance, beginning at the point where you began to experience the inaccurate or questionable results.

STEP 2: CHECKING DONNA'S MAIN POINTS

Read the following statements one at a time and do Muscle Checking with a Partner, Self Muscle Checking, or Noticing to determine if your body is switched-on or switched-off after saying each statement. If you are Muscle Checking with a Partner, read each statement out loud. Place a check mark next to any statements for which you are switched-off:

_____ 1. "I follow through when I have thoughts of gratitude and sincerely express my appreciation to others."

_____ 2. "I am comfortable giving and receiving acknowledgements."

_____ 3. "I stay in contact with people, keeping the lines of communication open."

_____ 4. "I am comfortable reconnecting with people even when I haven't talked to them in quite a while."

_____ 5. "It is easy for me to be friendly, considerate, and helpful when I am networking."

STEP 3. IDENTIFYING TRIGGER POINTS FOR YOURSELF:

In the chart below, write down any statements from Donna's material (that aren't already listed above), that triggered an uncomfortable or negative response for you. In the right-hand column, write out your positive goal regarding the Trigger Point you identified. Muscle Check with a Partner, Self Muscle Check or Notice on both the negative side (Trigger Point) and the positive goal side of what you wrote. If you are Muscle Checking with a Partner, read the statements out loud. If you are switched off, then place a check mark by that Trigger Point. If you find that you are switched-on for the Trigger Point and positive goal statement, then what you thought was a negative Trigger Point is not one.

TRIGGER POINTS	POSITIVE GOAL STATEMENTS

If you are switched-on for all of Donna's Main Points and you did not identify any Trigger Points for yourself, then you don't have any major issues or difficulties with the information in this chapter. If this is the case, skip to Step 6 and do the Brain Gym movements and exercises listed there. By doing the Brain Gym exercises and movements even though you are already switched-on, you may achieve an even higher level of networking success.

STEP 4. ACTIONS

Now do a physical activity, role play, or visualization for at least twenty seconds for each of Donna's Main Points and for the Trigger Points you were switched-off for in Steps 2 and 3. Do Muscle Checking with a Partner, Self Muscle Checking, or Noticing for the actions as soon as you complete each one and place a check mark next to each action for which you are switched-off.

STEP 5. CHOOSING TO INCLUDE THE PAST:

Say to yourself (or out loud to your partner, if you are working with a partner): "My system now incorporates, in the most appropriate way, all relevant past events, known and unknown, into my experience." Now do Muscle Checking with a Partner, Self Muscle Checking, or Noticing for a "yes" or "no" response. (See page 45 for an explanation of a "yes" or "no" response.)

STEP 6. TAKING ACTION: Doing the Brain Gym Movements

Now is the time to do the Brain Gym Movements listed below:
- The Cross Crawl (see page 65)
- Arm Activation (see page 60)
- Belly Breathing (see page 61)
- Hook-ups (see page 63)
- The Positive Points (see page 69)
- Brain Buttons (see page 61)
- Earth Buttons (see page 62)
- The Grounder (see page 67)
- Lazy 8s (see page 63)

STEP 7. CHECKING DONNA'S MAIN POINTS AND YOUR TRIGGER POINTS

Now you're going to recheck the statements from Steps 2 and 3 to make sure you are switched-on for all of the Statements. If you are doing Muscle Checking with a Partner read the statements out loud, or do Self Muscle Checking, or Noticing.

1. "I follow through when I have thoughts of gratitude and sincerely express my appreciation to others."
2. "I am comfortable giving and receiving acknowledgements."
3. "I stay in contact with people, keeping the lines of communication open."
4. "I am comfortable reconnecting with people even when I haven't talked to them in quite a while."
5. "It is easy for me to be friendly, considerate, and helpful when I am networking."

Repeat the Actions that you did in Step 4, doing each of them for at least twenty seconds. This time when you do the action, you will find that you are switched-on for it. It will be easier to do and you will be able to do it with less stress.

STEP 8. WHERE ARE YOU NOW?

Now that you've completed the Balance for Nurturing Your Network, it's time to reassess your level of improvement or change from your responses to the questionnaire on page 96. You'll find the questions that relate to this particular Balance below.

Place a check mark in the column on the right that most clearly reflects your level of agreement or disagreement with each statement below. Then compare your current response with your initial response. Additionally, I urge you to mark your calendar and re-check your responses a month from now to assess your continued improvement. Many people find that their improvement level increases even more a month later.

	Strongly Disagree	Disagree	Doesn't Apply	Agree	Strongly Agree
7. I enjoy nurturing my network by giving of my time and energy.					
8. I am comfortable and confident acknowledging people and expressing my appreciation.					
9. I know I am a valuable resource for others.					

STEP 9. IT'S TIME TO CELEBRATE

If you're Self Muscle Checking or Noticing, congratulate yourself. If you're working with a partner, celebrate the successful completion of the Balance for Nurturing Your Network and switching yourself on.

STEP 10. REINFORCING THE BALANCE WITH HOME PLAY

Each time you finish reading and doing the Balances for the day, there's one more step before you end your Switched-On Networking session. Home play gives you the opportunity to reinforce and enhance the re-wiring and rebalancing in the brain if your mind-body feels it would be beneficial to do so. Go to Chapter 14 on page 231 and follow the directions there.

NOTE: If you are continuing to work in this current session, skip this step, and go on to the next chapter. Then, after you complete the last Balance you plan to do for the day, go to Chapter 14 and do the Home Play.

CHAPTER 10

CONNECTING ONLINE
AND FACE-TO-FACE

Identify Statements for Balance Section:

As you read through Donna's section below, be aware of any discomfort or negativity that comes to mind about the specific suggestions she makes. Make note of these responses and, when you get to the balance, if those issues are not covered, you'll have the opportunity to write them down.

In the truest sense of the phrase, the world is a networking event. Any time people are interacting anywhere—online or face-to-face—the potential for networking is present. It is through those interactions—those conversations—that we create new networking relationships and discover how to be resources for one another. This is why it is so important to realize that networking is a lifestyle and way of relating to people—no matter where you are. Anywhere there are two or more people in conversation networking can happen—meaning people connect, share information, and support one another in some way.

Although networking can happen anywhere, there are a multitude of events organized specifically for the purpose of giving people a place to come together to meet, mingle, and make valuable connections. These events are typically sponsored by chambers of commerce, industry associations, trade shows, professional networking clubs, community organizations, religious and spiritual groups, alumni associations, and corporations. People participate for a variety of reasons—the camaraderie, social interaction, job leads, political advancement, and prospecting for business.

Your Online Neighborhood

In a relatively short period of time, the Internet has become the world's venue for shopping, getting an education, finding a job, finding a mate, starting a revolution, networking and more. You may think the power of the future lies with technology. After all, technology influences our lives every day—and it does so in major ways. However, the truth is that the power of technology lies with people and how people choose to use it to enhance their lives and the communities and world within which we live. The venues and opportunities for networking online are numerous and evolving rapidly as technology creates new options. Whether you find people to connect with via Facebook, Meetup. com, a LinkedIn group, Twitter, or one of many other online sites, the opportunity is yours.

Sometimes a computer, a smart phone and access to the Internet is all someone requires to start and grow a successful business—no need for an office, lobby, conference room, or neon sign—and, voila, we now have access to millions of people. And the people we have access to online can easily be identified as prospects, vendors, affiliates, potential employees, or people who share the same interests and desires.

At one time in our culture people lived in neighborhoods where everyone knew everyone else. People would often do business with the same businesses their whole life; sometimes even for generations. Children and grandchildren would continue to go to the same doctor, or dentist, or call on the same plumber or furnace repairman. Networking was not even something we had to think about or give much attention to; it was built into the lifestyle.

However, in recent times people move more; many don't know their neighbors well enough to even say a passing "hello." People change jobs, homes, partners, doctors, dentists, and other providers on a more frequent basis than ever. And yet, what has stayed the same in the midst of all this change is our inherent desire to have a sense of community and belonging. This is one reason the social networking sites are so popular. Online communities give people the experience of being connected and part of a community.

Through the Internet's social media sites, we can stay connected with people—no matter where they live or how many times they move. Instead of just having neighborhoods defined by geography, we now have online communities that have no geographical boundaries at all. Technology is now integrated into our lifestyle through our computers, smart phones, iPads and other new devices and programs that provide 24/7 connectivity.

Having people in your life that you know, that you can call on and count on is a basic human desire. Having a sense of connectedness is important to your mental health, physical well-being, and personal success. Networking is about taking responsibility for developing your community of support.

Ask yourself:
- What can I do to create a more connected community—online and face-to-face?
- What can I do through online activity to keep connected with friends and clients who live throughout the world?
- What can I do to lessen the isolation in my life and, instead, create an even stronger sense of connection?
- What can I do to make sure that the bonds that I create with my personal friends and professional colleagues can stand up to the challenges of a busy, fast-paced culture?

Blending the Basics of Face-to-Face and Online Networking

The skills that make for good face-to-face networking make for good online networking. Networking is about relationship building and the basics are the same, whether you're networking online or offline; with men or women; in a setting that is urban or suburban, global or local; and whether you're working or job-seeking.

Diane Darling, author of *The Networking Survival Guide,* refers to the blend of face-to-face and online networking as hybrid networking. Hybrid networking happens when you weave back and forth from online to face-to-face interactions. With a hybrid car sometimes you are running on gas and sometimes on electricity. With hybrid networking you participate in both online and offline activities. "Digital relationships" are strengthened by also having interactions in other venues—phone-to-phone, Skype, video conferencing, and face-to-face.

The same basic concepts of etiquette apply online as they do in the real world, including common courtesy. In fact, online it's more important than ever to understand and respect the difference between networking and selling. When the purpose of an event or a social media site is to network, an attempt to "sell" can be counter-productive. If you incessantly promote yourself, your products, and your services on your social media sites, it is easier than ever for people to simply "disconnect" from you or even worse admonish you publicly online for your behavior.

> *Networking works, no matter what the venue, as long as people are connecting and sharing resources respectfully.*

Just as the etiquette of networking is the same online as it is face-to-face, the benefits are also every bit as real. Online networking does provide some additional benefits, as outlined below:

Additional Benefits of Online Networking
- **Ultra-targeting**
  Online networking gives you the means to target a specific group of people. Just as there are associations and conferences for every industry and interest group you can imagine, there are ultra-focused online sites. Find an online community where the people you are looking for are already gathering. And if you can't find the type of community you're looking for, then start one.
- **Time-efficiency**
  A major concern about online networking is how time consuming it can be and yet it's just like face-to-face networking. You have control over the amount of time you spend online and it is up to you to make your participation on the

social media sites useful, valuable, and productive. You can also use software and apps that allow you to post to all your social media sites at the same time as a way to be more time-efficient.

- **Connecting across time zones and geographic lines**
  With online networking you can connect with people across all time zones and geographical lines while doing so at the time and place of yours and their choosing.

- **Reaching the masses**
  Grow your online network and you can reach the masses with your postings as they are passed along from person to person and from one community to another. The example would be retweeting a tweet that you like. At the same time many sites also give you the ability to send private messages and create one-on-one chatting scenarios.

- **Freedom and flexibility of networking when it is convenient for you**
  You choose your schedule. Whether you are a "night owl" or an "early bird" or an "all nighter" the internet is available 24/7 so that you network when it works for you.

- **Communicating with people you would not normally have access to**
  In the past people could "hide" behind receptionists and administrators in order to determine how they can be accessed. Now more and more people are making themselves available through online sites allowing for communications that would have been difficult if not impossible in the past.

- **Reconnecting with people you might have lost touch with**
  Online profiles provide you and others with information that allows you to reconnect with people from your hometown, your high school, college, sorority or fraternity, former places of employment, military organizations, and professional associations and organizations.

- **Increased visibility and enhanced online traffic**
  Inter-linking your website, blog, videos, fundraising page, shopping cart, and online profiles creates a strong internet presence for you and gives people an easy path to follow to learn more about you, your products and your services.
- **Access to vast amounts of information**
  You can easily get to know more about individuals, companies, organizations, and industries by searching for them online and reviewing information posted about them on their online profiles and other related Internet sites.
- **Word-of-*mouse* marketing**
  I refer to the modern version of word-of-mouth marketing as "word-of-***mouse***" marketing because a single click of a mouse can send a message that could potentially reach millions. The immediacy of online messaging and posting on social media sites makes it easy for people to pass along information—including positive or negative comments—to their online network in real time, while they are at stores, restaurants, conferences, events, etc.

Virtual Networking—The Ultimate Mingle

Whether you enjoy the process of mingling with others at in-person networking events or not, I think you'll find that taking part in a virtual networking event is the ultimate in mingling with ease. Connections are made while you're comfortably ensconced in your home or office. You are there to connect with people and network and so is everyone else. Everyone participates equally and benefits equally and resources are shared easily and efficiently.

Just think—with virtual networking you don't spend time getting ready and driving to an event. And you don't have to have business cards handy or summon the courage to walk up to someone new or approach a group of people who are already interacting. In virtual networking events you simply call in at the appointed time and are placed—over the phone—in a group of three to four people with a several minutes for everyone to introduce themselves and network with each other.

Then you are placed in another group of three to four people. And so on as you continue to network with additional groups for the duration of the virtual networking event.

Sign up for a virtual networking event at www.TheMingleGroup. com or www.NetworkingJam.com and experience the ease of making new connections in a virtual venue. You can also sign up to schedule and host your own virtual networking event and invite the people in your network to connect with each other virtually. Virtual events can be a great adjunct to regularly scheduled in-person meetings of associations, chambers, and professional networking groups, giving members additional opportunities to connect with each other.

Mental Preparation

When going to a "networking event," a little preparation can go a long way. And mainly what I'm talking about here is mental preparation— even if you simply take a moment to focus on the event while you're on your way to an in-person event or right before you log onto an online event. Think about:

- **What type of event you are attending?**
  Think about the purpose of the event. Is it strictly about networking or is there also a theme or program that influences how people will be interacting?
- **Who is sponsoring the event?**
  Is the event being sponsored by a company you already do business with—or one that you would like to connect with in the future? Do you already know any of the individuals who are involved with the sponsorship? What can you do or say to express your appreciation to them for the opportunities the event presents for you?
- **Who do you already know who will be attending the event?**
  Take a moment to recall what you know about the individuals who are likely to attend and think about how you might initiate conversations and also connect their business interests to yours.

- **Who is likely to be attending the event who you are most interested in meeting?**
  Are there people whom you are especially interested in meeting because they can be a great connection for you and/or because you can be a great resource for them? Who will be attending the event who can introduce you to the people you desire to meet?
- **Who invited you?**
  Be sure to connect with the person who invited you to say hello and thank her for inviting you.
- **What is your "introduction statement"?**
  Take a moment to think about your "introduction statement." What do you most desire for people to know about your business? Is there a particular project or new product or recent accomplishment that you are focused on and are ready to tell people about? Are you looking for a specific resource or contact that someone at the event can possibly help you with?
- **What is your purpose for participating in this particular event?**
  Think about your purpose for participating in this event. There are numerous reasons you may decide to attend:
  - It's been a busy week in the office and you are ready to get out and socialize with people.
  - This is a group of people you particularly enjoy and choose to stay connected with.
  - You are looking for a particular resource and believe that this venue could be a place to make that connection.
  - The sponsor of the event is an important contact in your network and you are going to be supportive of that person.
  - It's important for you to be visible and known within this group and so you choose to show up.
  - It's a new group and you are curious and are interested in finding out what it's all about.
  - It's a group that has supported you; therefore, you desire to participate as an opportunity to express your appreciation and give back.

Whatever your reason for attending, by prepping your mind, you will more easily and confidently participate, generate interactions, and connect with people in an easy, natural, and effective manner.

Supplies for Face-to-Face Events

Face-to-Face networking doesn't really require much in terms of supplies because it's all about you and at least one other person having a conversation. And yet, there are certain items that are important to keep on hand and have easily reachable.

- **Your business cards**

  Keep your business cards handy so that when someone asks for your card you can get to it easily. Ideally, if you have a jacket pocket on the side that is opposite of your dominant hand, that is an ideal place to keep your business cards. That way, when it's time to give someone a card, it is very easy to reach with your dominate hand into the pocket on your opposite side and pull out a card.

  When someone hands you their business card take a moment to read the card. While this conveys respect, it's also helpful for networking because you may find something interesting on the card to comment on or ask about. Plus, by reading someone's card on the spot, you are reinforcing that person's information into your memory for later recall.

  The main thing is make your business card exchange a natural part of your conversation. There will be a place in the conversation where it is very natural to ask for their card or offer your card.

- **Pen**

  Having a pen **handy**—not deep in the bottom of a purse or briefcase—is great for those moments when you choose to write a quick note to yourself regarding one of your networking conversations. The note might be a reminder about the conversation you had with the person or it could be a reminder about something you promised to do as a result of your conversation, such as sending an email, mailing a brochure, scheduling a meeting, sending information on a referral you are recommending, etc.

- **Brochures, Flyers, and Resumes**
  Some people like to have brochures and flyers and even, when appropriate, resumes to hand out when they're networking. However, unless you're in a situation that calls for those items, I recommend that you save them to follow up with later. My experience is that most people have a place to put business cards when they are networking, but they don't necessarily have a place to store other documents and it may be inconvenient for them to hold on to them.

To Mingle Or Not to Mingle

The purpose of a networking mixer is to mingle, which means "to mix, to associate or take part with others, to participate." Even if you are at an event that is not a mixer, such as a workshop, open house, or party, it is always a good idea to mingle. Some events are strictly mingle-type environments where you are on your own to meet people, while others are specifically set up for "speed networking" with individuals circulating from table to table for set periods of time. A variation of speed networking is provided in some virtual networking events, which as I've mentioned provides for circulation from group to group online instead of face-to-face. Although the principles of networking have been consistent over time, technology and creativity continue to lead to new, efficient ways to connect with people.

You Make the Difference by Putting People at Ease

Whether it's an official networking event or simply a neighborhood pool party, a wedding reception or a company picnic, any social event you attend can lead to valuable information, contacts, and opportunities. Some people find social events uncomfortable, time-consuming, and unproductive while others view them as fun, productive, and valuable opportunities. What makes the difference? *You* make the difference in each and every networking situation with your attitude, your communication skills, your ability to engage in small talk that's interesting and fun instead of boring and dull, and your ability to listen.

Most people feel uncomfortable walking into a room full of people. Typically that's because they are focused on themselves. When you take your attention off yourself and focus on putting others at ease, your self-consciousness will disappear. Switched-on-networkers are confident in their ability to mingle with ease by putting other people at ease. Instead of worrying about what you're going to say; focus on what others are saying. Instead of being concerned about whether someone's going to talk with you, reach out to someone and initiate a conversation.

When you feel at ease, people will be comfortable around you. Make it easy for people to approach you. If you have a scowl on your face, crossed arms, rigid posture, and appear aloof, people will keep their distance. That type of body language will steer even the most enthusiastic people away. On the other hand, if you want to make yourself approachable, you can invite people in with your open posture, natural eye contact, and relaxed smile. The more relaxed and at ease you feel, the more you'll be likely to have a good time and make some solid connections. Networking simply happens through conversation, yet someone has to be willing to reach out and initiate the conversation. That someone can be you! Networking is meant to be fun and easy and it can be when you relax and allow yourself to mingle with ease.

The Truth About Small Talk

Many people cringe at the thought of what is referred to as "small talk" because the word "small" implies little, insignificant, and minor. People think of small talk as meaningless because there is no goal or end result to be accomplished—therefore, it can seem frivolous. However, small talk is not insignificant chit-chat. It lays the groundwork for relationships, giving people the opportunity to get to know one another in a safe and non-threatening manner. Small talk opens the door to conversation so that opportunities and interests can be discovered. Done in a smart way, it leads to quality conversations which, in turn, lead to information, ideas, and relationships that add richness to your life. So, lets start calling it smart talk!

Smart talk is the exploratory stage in conversation that leads to discovering commonalities and opportunities—and conversation is where networking happens. When you focus on putting people at ease and show an interest in learning more about others, small talk leads to connection, trust, and rapport. Have you ever noticed yourself in a conversation that seems to be going nowhere? Then all of a sudden you find that you have something in common with the other person and the conversation takes off.

Networking is not about *making* people talk or cornering people on elevators, but about your ability to open the door to conversation with the people right around you. Most people are waiting on someone else to make the conversation interesting. Remember, you have the power to direct your conversations to topics that are of interest and value to the people you are talking with. Opportunities exist all around you; wherever people are, networking is possible.

When people ask questions, respond in a conversational manner with information that leads to further interaction. Keep a dialogue going, not a monologue. Don't talk on and on about yourself. Listen for phrases such as "I want," "I need," "I'm looking for," and then think about your own network to see if there's a name, idea, or information you can offer.

When you take the time to listen and get to know someone, there is almost always some basis for relating and networking. The mistake we sometimes make is to think that we already know people rather than taking the time to learn something new about them and thus get to know them even better. Instead of asking the typical question, "How are you doing?" or "What's new?" ask questions that are intriguing and open ended. Ask questions that generate conversation, such as, "You said your work involves ... tell me more about that" or "You mentioned ... I'm interested in hearing more" or "When you said you do ... what does that mean?"

Explore with your conversations. Listen well and gather information and you will walk away from every conversation richer—in terms of information and the connections that you make with people.

The Balance Between Talking and Listening

In our society people are hungry to be heard. Because so many people are busy talking and telling others what to do and think, few people are feeling really "heard." When you truly listen to people and they feel "heard," they are more likely to trust you and share more information with you. In order for people to feel heard, you must realize that listening is not simply a matter of not talking. Listening that generates trust and relationship is about being mentally engaged in what the other person is saying.

People can sense when you are truly listening and when you are only feigning interest. You show that you care by the way you listen because the process of listening conveys sincerity and attention. You can become a great conversationalist simply by strengthening your listening skills. Strong listening skills will also increase your effectiveness and ability to retain and remember information better so that you can follow up more effectively later. When you are listening and paying attention to what people are saying, you will discover commonalities and ways you can be of support to one another. And listening is a great conversational tool; people will say things you can naturally comment on, thus generating an easy, natural conversational flow.

Masterful listening means giving your full attention to someone else to create a connection that goes beyond the words that are being said. It is through listening that people connect and develop trust and rapport. Listening is about more than just hearing the words. It is about connecting.

Don't Drop the Connection

Online and face-to-face events give you the opportunity to connect with people; and yet making connections is just the start of the networking process. Follow up and follow through activities make the difference in both developing relationships and creating results. And yet, if you don't have systems in place to support you in following through and staying in touch with people, the value of the initial connection can be lost. Your follow through is just as important as your initial participation in online and face-to-face networking events.

Follow-up Systems

- By having systems in place, you are much more likely to take the "follow-through" steps that are key to having the time you spend networking lead to worthwhile results. Writing a personal note to someone and having it printed and mailed for you can take as little as 30 seconds using the technology that's now available online for sending cards to people in your network. Create your own online account for sending notecards at http://www.NetworkingWithKindness.com. Systems can simplify your life and your networking process. Systems work when you work the systems that are available to you.
- Keep track of contact information on your computer, using software that's easily searchable. That way, if you forget a person's name or company, you can search for that person by city, state, organization, industry, or other criteria.
- Keep a calendar on your phone and/or computer to track appointments, events, etc.
- Use an email system with features for sending both individual emails and group emails (for people who have requested information from you).

Follow-up Guidelines

- Be prompt in following up with people after you meet and/or reconnect with them.
- Follow up can be with a card, email, social media posting, text message, or phone call depending on the situation. When following up, remind the person of when you last talked with them and what prompted the follow up.
- If you offered to get back to someone regarding something you talked about, do so promptly.
- If you get busy and forget to get back with someone, go ahead and follow through as soon as you remember. Even late follow up is better than no follow through at all. "I apologize for taking so long to get back with you about …. Here is …." People will appreciate your follow through even if your response was slower than ideal.

Networking Clubs: Are They for You?

If you are an entrepreneur, business owner, and/or sole proprietor, joining a professional networking club is recommended. Why? These groups provide camaraderie and support that can be essential in making wise decisions about your business, in maintaining the motivation and perspective that keeps you on track with your business, and in developing a support system that provides access to the products and services that will enhance your business.

The central theme around a networking club meeting is helping to build and improve the businesses of the members. As a member of a professional networking club, you will meet other professionals and other business owners easily and naturally as the club grows. A networking club provides an environment that encourages you to network because members are expected to participate by mentoring each other, providing an excellent business and entrepreneurial training ground. Imagine having 20 to 40 mentors who are close by and choose to help each other.

Why Join a Networking Club?
- Increase your revenues
- Develop business relationships
- Obtain business ideas and support
- Gain broad perspective as a business owner
- Place yourself in a networking environment
- Gain from the advice and experience of other business professionals
- Camaraderie
- Get easy access to services of other professionals
- Cultivate long term contacts
- Expand your network since your network automatically grows as the club grows
- Education and professional development provided by speakers at meetings who provide information on business, educational, and community topics

Mental Roadblocks to Joining a Professional Networking Club

Does joining a networking club feel like just one more commitment in a too-busy schedule? Let's look at some of the mental roadblocks you might have:

- Too early, not a morning person
- Too expensive, can't afford it
- Don't have time
- Don't feel that the members would be viable prospects for my business
- Already have enough business, don't need any leads
- Don't see the value

Now let's evaluate these concerns by looking at the merits versus the downsides:

Too early, not a morning person:

It's true that many networking clubs meet for breakfast before the work day starts. If you give it a chance, you may find it's worth adjusting your schedule for that early morning meeting and also find that an entrepreneurial support group is a great way to get your day started. However, there are also plenty of networking clubs that meet in the midday or evening. So find a group that works for you and your schedule. The energy, support, and enthusiasm of this type of group can provide an energy boost that you may not get anywhere else.

Too expensive, can't afford it:

Joining an entrepreneurial support group is about making an investment and a commitment to your business. You are not just paying for meals or paying for a membership. You are investing in building a support team that will provide business, feedback, ideas, and support that is worth many times more than the actual membership fees.

Don't have time:
Most clubs meet for one hour or possibly an hour and a half once a week or twice a month. Don't think of this as just a social gathering. This is possibly the most cost effective and valuable marketing and business development time you can dedicate to your business.

Don't feel that the members would be viable prospects for my business:
Each member has their own vast network of contacts. So even if members may not be a prospect for your business, they will know people who are prospects. And every member can be of support by providing business ideas, feedback, and support regarding various aspects of your business.

Already have enough business. Don't need any leads:
Congratulations and good for you if your business is full and booming. However, it is always wise to develop a support system and continue to "water the tree" and do things that contribute to the ongoing growth and success of your business.

Don't see the value:
There is great intrinsic value in the friendships, professional relationships, ease of access to information and contacts as well as the benefit of additional business opportunities.

Create What Works for You

Linda Starr and I facilitate a once-a-month meeting in Houston for women. This group was borne out of my desire to meet with like-minded, supportive women and to allow the group to be "organic" and grow on its own. I wanted it to be easy and inclusive (no membership, no criteria) so women could easily connect with and receive the support of other women. In the format that we use, each woman is invited to briefly introduce herself. Then we invite the attendees to share announcements, requests, and acknowledgements.

In addition to monthly meetings, participants also connect via our Facebook page (www.FaceBook.com/c3women) and use our Yahoo group to make announcements, requests, and acknowledgements in between our face-to-face meetings. Many networking clubs now use some combination of face-to-face meetings and online sites to make it easy to connect and share information with one another.

Participation Is Key!

I have seen people join a club, group, or chamber and expect the members to immediately line up to be their customers. That could happen but generally it takes a bit of time to build trust and rapport through your participation. Follow the principles of networking – giving, listening, and being a resource and results will start to show over time.

A networking club addresses the human desire to connect with others, to feel a sense of belonging, to be part of something bigger than ourselves. A networking club provides you with a team, a professional family. A networking club can be an incredible life-enchanter and business builder.

BALANCE FOR CONNECTING ONLINE AND FACE-TO-FACE

In this Balance, you will educate your brain to effectively, comfortably, and even enjoyably network with the people you are meeting online and face-to-face.

STEP 1. CALIBRATION: Preparing for the Process

If necessary, refer to the more detailed instructions on Calibration on page 71.

1. **Water and Hydration:** To make sure you are well hydrated, drink some water.

2. **Electrical Circuitry:** To make sure your electrical circuitry is operating efficiently, do Brain Buttons (page 61).

3. **Activating:** To make sure your body is ready to move, do The Cross Crawl (page 65).

4. **Stress Reduction:** To make sure your stress response is deactivated, do Hook-ups (page 63).

5. **Method to Use:** Select whether you will do Muscle Checking with a Partner, Self Muscle Checking, or Noticing (page 39 to 54). (View online muscle checking demonstrations at www.SwitchedOnNetworking.com/demo.)

6. **"Yes"/"No" Response:** Use the biofeedback response method you chose to ask your body for a "yes" and then a "no" response (page 45).

NOTE: When you are in the middle of a Balance, it's possible you may begin to get inaccurate or questionable results. While this rarely occurs, it is a possibility. In case it does occur, simply repeat the Calibration procedure, and then proceed with the Balance, beginning at the point where you began to experience the inaccurate or questionable results.

STEP 2: CHECKING DONNA'S MAIN POINTS

Read the following statements one at a time and do Muscle Checking with a Partner, Self Muscle Checking, or Noticing to determine if your body is switched-on or switched-off after saying each statement. If you are Muscle Checking with a Partner, read each statement out loud. Place a check mark next to any statements for which you are switched-off:

_____ 1. "I easily and effectively build relationships with the people I connect with both online and face-to-face."

_____ 2. "I respect the people participating in online communities by posting messages that are relevant."

_____ 3. "I use the Internet professionally and appropriately in connecting with people and marketing my business worldwide."

_____ 4. "I am comfortable balancing the time I spend on face-to-face and online networking activities."

_____ 5. "I mingle with ease and enjoy meeting new people at networking events."

_____ 6. "I listen to what people are saying and easily engage in conversations."

STEP 3. IDENTIFYING TRIGGER POINTS FOR YOURSELF:

In the chart below, write down any statements from Donna's material (that aren't already listed above), that triggered an uncomfortable or negative response for you. In the right-hand column, write out your positive goal regarding the Trigger Point you identified. Muscle Check with a Partner, Self Muscle Check or Notice on both the negative side (Trigger Point) and the positive goal side of what you wrote. If you are Muscle Checking with a Partner, read the statements out loud. If you are switched off, then place a check mark by that Trigger Point. If you find that you are switched-on for the Trigger Point and positive goal statement, then what you thought was a negative Trigger Point is not one.

TRIGGER POINTS	POSITIVE GOAL STATEMENTS
_____	_____
_____	_____
_____	_____
_____	_____
_____	_____
_____	_____
_____	_____
_____	_____

If you are switched-on for all of Donna's Main Points and you did not identify any Trigger Points for yourself, then you don't have any major issues or difficulties with the information in this chapter. If this is the case, skip to Step 6 and do the Brain Gym movements and exercises listed there. By doing the Brain Gym exercises and movements even though you are already switched-on, you may achieve an even higher level of networking success.

STEP 4. ACTIONS

Now do a physical activity, role play, or visualization for at least twenty seconds for each of Donna's Main Points and for the Trigger Points you were switched-off for in Steps 2 and 3. Do Muscle Checking with a Partner, Self Muscle Checking, or Noticing for the actions as soon as you complete each one and place a check mark next to each action for which you are switched-off.

STEP 5. CHOOSING TO INCLUDE THE PAST:

Say to yourself (or out loud to your partner, if you are working with a partner): "My system now incorporates, in the most appropriate way, all relevant past events, known and unknown, into my experience." Now do Muscle Checking with a Partner, Self Muscle Checking, or Noticing for a "yes" or "no" response. (See page 45 for an explanation of a "yes" or "no" response.)

STEP 6. TAKING ACTION: Doing the Brain Gym Movements

Now's the time for you to do the Brain Gym movements listed below. (See the instructions and illustrations for each of the Brain Gym movements in Chapter 4 beginning on page 57.)
- The Cross Crawl (see page 65)
- The Grounder (see page 67)
- The Calf Pump (see page 65)
- The Owl (see page 68)
- Belly Breathing (see page 61)

- The Positive Points (see page 69)
- Hook-ups (see page 63)
- Lazy 8s (see page 63)
- The Thinking Cap (see page 69)

STEP 7. CHECKING DONNA'S MAIN POINTS AND YOUR TRIGGER POINTS

Now you're going to recheck the statements from Steps 2 and 3 to make sure you are switched-on for all of the Statements. If you are doing Muscle Checking with a Partner read the statements out loud, or do Self Muscle Checking, or Noticing.

1. "I easily and effectively build relationships with the people I connect with both online and face-to-face."
2. "I respect the people participating in online communities by posting messages that are relevant."
3. "I use the Internet professionally and appropriately in connecting with people and marketing my business worldwide."
4. "I am comfortable balancing the time I spend on face-to-face and online networking activities."
5. "I mingle with ease and enjoy meeting new people at networking events."
6. "I listen to what people are saying and easily engage in conversations."

Repeat the Actions that you did in Step 4, doing each of them for at least twenty seconds. This time when you do the action, you will find that you are switched-on for it. It will be easier to do and you will be able to do it with less stress.

STEP 8. WHERE ARE YOU NOW?

Now that you've completed the Balance for Connecting Online and Face-to-Face, it's time to reassess your level of improvement or change from your responses to the questionnaire you originally filled out on page 96. You'll find the questions that relate to this particular Balance below.

Place a check mark in the column on the right that most clearly reflects your level of agreement or disagreement with each statement below. Then compare your current response with your initial response. Additionally, I urge you to mark your calendar and re-check your responses a month from now to assess your continued improvement. Many people find that their improvement level increases even further a month later.

		Strongly Disagree	Disagree	Doesn't Apply	Agree	Strongly Agree
10.	I am comfortable connecting with people through online and offline activities.					
11.	I am comfortable and confident attending networking events.					
12.	I feel confident introducing myself to new people.					
13.	I easily and effectively develop my online presence.					

STEP 9. IT'S TIME TO CELEBRATE

If you're Self Muscle Checking or Noticing, congratulate yourself. If you're working with a partner, celebrate the successful completion of the Balance for Connecting and switching yourself on.

STEP 10. REINFORCING THE BALANCE WITH HOME PLAY

Each time you finish reading and doing the Balances for the day, there's one more step before you end your Switched-On Networking session. Home play gives you the opportunity to reinforce and enhance the re-wiring and rebalancing in the brain if your mind-body feels it would be beneficial to do so. Go to Chapter 14 on page 231 and follow the directions there.

NOTE: If you are continuing to work in this current session, skip this step, and go on to the next chapter. Then, after you complete the last Balance you plan to do for the day, go to Chapter 14 and do the Home Play.

CHAPTER 11

UPGRADING YOUR CONVERSATIONS

Identifying Statements for Balance Section:

As you read through Donna's section below, be aware of any discomfort or negativity that comes to mind about the specific suggestions she makes. Make note of these responses and, when you get to the balance, if those issues are not covered, you'll have the opportunity to write them down.

Whether you are networking in person, by phone, or online, your conversation is key to creating the results you desire. Networking happens through conversation and you are responsible for whether a conversation turns into idle chit-chat or leads to a fruitful and interesting exchange of information. *What* you say can open the door to an opportunity that will make a difference for you—and for your world. In every conversation you have the opportunity to connect, inspire, and empower yourself and others.

Look at the world of marketing and you'll see how our words make a difference. Think about how much time and money business people spend choosing their business name, web address, tag line, or slogan. Marketing experts are hired to come up with the most effective word, phrase, and marketing piece. The specific words you use influence your environment and the people around you—your network. Words matter. And your words matter because you matter.

One Word Makes a Difference

Upgrading your conversations involves *consciously* choosing your words. You may have, in the past, spoken automatically and unconsciously without realizing that some of your words and phrases were disempowering. You are creating your world through your conversations. With new information you can make new choices.

One word can make a difference in being *clear,* rather than vague; *confident,* rather than hesitant; and *assertive,* rather than aggressive. You will have a chance here to become aware of words that convey a different message and energy than you intend so that you can upgrade to create empowering connections with people. Jerry's Brain Gym Balance in this chapter will assist you in integrating new word choices into your networking conversations.

Asking "Who Do You know?"

You may already know the importance of asking an open-ended question (rather than a closed-ended question) when networking. When asking for contacts, ask "**Who** do you know who... ?" rather than "**Do** you know anyone who... ?"

"**Do** you know anyone who ...?" is a closed-ended question that's easy for people to respond to with a simple "yes" or "no". An automatic "no" response happens when someone doesn't even take the time to scroll through his mental rolodex to find an answer to your question. On the other hand, when you ask "**Who** do you know who ...?" you are asking people to scroll through their "mental database" to find the contact who fits your request.

> *Switch from "Do you know anyone who ...?"*
> *to "WHO do you know who ...?"*

Announcements Versus Requests

In networking scenarios, you may hear comments like, "I'm looking for people who..." and "I'm looking for a contact in XYZ industry." It may seem like a request, but it's actually an announcement. Unless people have trained themselves to "think like a resource," they may simply hear the information without even thinking of responding. Just like salespeople are trained to ask for the sale, *in networking it is important to ask for the support or the information—make your request.*

Turning announcements into requests is easy when you add a "**Who** do you know" question and give people a chance to actually respond. Here are some examples of specific requests:

- "I am looking for… **Who** do you recommend I contact?"
- "I am looking for… **Who** do you know who could be a resource for me?"

Notice that the first sentence in each of the examples above is an announcement—and it ends with a period. That's okay as long as it is followed by a question that actually calls for a response.

Switch from an announcement to a request by adding a question:
"Who do you recommend?", "Who do you suggest?",
"Who do you know who… ?"

Do It or Don't Do It—Letting Go of "Trying"

Being credible and accountable creates an important level of trust in your networking relationships. People are most likely to call on people they know they can count on to do what they say they're going to do. Although the word "try" may sometimes be spoken with good intentions, it is a disempowering word that often adds confusion—instead of clarity—to a relationship.

When you are networking and someone tells you, "I'll *try* to get back with you by next Friday," what impression are you left with? Are they going to get back to you by Friday or not? Can you count on them or not? When the word *try* is used, neither person feels connected or empowered by the conversation because of the ambiguous nature of what's actually being said.

The word *try* does not really indicate that something is going to get done. In fact, it implies that it's *not* going to get done. "Try" actually means "to make an attempt" and "attempt" means to "make an effort" and yet there is nothing in either definition about "doing" or "accomplishing." People sabotage their networking relationships when they say they will "try" rather than truly making a commitment to do something.

So what's a better choice? Say what you *are* going to do and then do it! Sounds simple right? Say what you'll do and do what you say and you will create trust and credibility in your networking relationships.

So what *can* you say if you are not able to do something—or if you're unsure about whether you will or not? Rather than saying, "Well, I'll *try* to do…" respond and say what you know you can do. If someone asks me to do something, I do have the option to respond with an honest "no" or with a counter offer. For example, let's say someone asks me to call everyone who attended our fundraising event by five p.m. on Friday. I have a busy schedule and getting all the phone calls done by then is questionable. So, taking *try* out of the equation, I can consider the options and then respond by making a commitment that works for me, such as, "I will call at least five people by five p.m. Friday and the rest by the end of the day on Monday."

Even an honest "no" is better than an ambiguous "try." In the above example, my response could be, "Getting in touch with everyone by five p.m. on Friday doesn't work for me. I request that you ask John if he can fit that in his schedule."

All of your networking and business relationships will benefit greatly if you avoid *trying* and speak honestly regarding what you will do.

Switch from "try" to: I am," "I can," "I will"

Choose to "Have"; Choose to Thrive!

The word "want" is commonly used in networking conversations when someone's making a request or expressing a desire. And yet what's important to realize is that the word *want* actually means "to be lacking" or "to be without." When you're saying "I *want* more customers," "I *want* to grow my business," or "I *want* to start my own business," the words *I want* creates more of the experience of *lacking* what you desire rather than creating what you desire.

As Robert Tennyson Stevens states in his book *Conscious Language™: The Logos of Now!,* "By saying 'want' we are agreeing to be in 'lack.' We all have the opportunity to hear ourselves say a limited statement and believe it or make a new choice."[17]

---

17 Stevens, Robert Tennyson, Conscious Language™: The Logos of Now!, Mastery Systems, 2007, page 77.

Make a new choice and upgrade from "want" to "I choose," "I claim," "I have," "I empower myself to have." Instead of saying, "I want to grow my business this year by 20 percent," I say, "I choose to grow my business this year by 20 percent."

"I would love to" and "I would like" are both similar to "I want." "I would like to" is more in line with "It would be nice" and "Maybe we could." Saying, "I would like to grow my business this year," is vague. When you say, "I choose to grown my business by 20% this year," you start to think differently, take actions, and behave according to your spoken outcome.

Another example of a "want" upgrade is saying, "Sara, I really want to get together with you." This statement expresses a want but it doesn't move either of us to action. The upgrade statement could be, "Sara, I request that we schedule a time to get together." Say the two sentences to yourself or out loud and notice the difference! Using the word "request" rather than "want" creates a power and intention behind my words that leads to action and fulfillment on my request.

People sometimes express concern that they will come across as weak or needy if they ask for help or support. And yet, making a clear request is very powerful and inspiring. Ask with conviction, clarity, and specificity, using the word "request" rather than "want" and people will experience and respond to your power.

Switch from "want" to: "I choose," "I request"

"Want" on Steroids

The word "need" is a more aggressive version of "want" and is used in networking conversations, as in "I need more business" or "I need more money" or "I need more clients." The root meaning of *need* is "violence" and "distress." As I thought about that, I realized that there is an energy and state of distress associated with the words, "I **need…**" or "I've **got to have**… ." An over-amped sense of "needing" something can lead to frustrating, unproductive, and destructive thoughts and behaviors. However, a clear, calm energy focused on attracting and claiming what you desire produces productive and inspiring ideas, actions, and behaviors.

I refer to "need" as "want" on steroids because it represents wanting in a way that is magnified. Upgrades from "need" and "want" include "I am finding new clients by attending networking events," "I choose to generate increased revenue by increasing my client base," or "I request your support in contacting the person in charge." To *want* and *need* is limiting and self sabotaging. To *choose* is power.

Switch from "need" to: "I choose," "I am", "I request"

Just the Facts, Please!

One of the principles of networking is to be specific. Whether you're introducing yourself or making a request, specificity can make the difference in making a solid connection. Being specific makes it easier for people to know how to respond in either situation. When you make a statement or request that is broad, vague, or grandiose, it's difficult for others to know exactly how to respond even though they have a desire to be of support.

Broad: "I'm looking for job leads."
Specific: "I am looking for contacts in Colorado in the energy industry."

Iffy: "I *might* be interested in talking with someone about my book idea."
Specific: "I am interested in talking with an agent about my cookbook idea."

Uncommitted: "If ever you're in New York, maybe we could get together."
Specific: "When you come to New York, I request an opportunity to meet with you."

Vague: "I'm *kind of* interested in connecting with people in XYZ industry to talk about career opportunities."

Specific: "I am connecting with people in the XYZ industry to explore how my engineering expertise fits with jobs in that industry."

Grandiose: "I work with people all over the world who want to be hugely successful."

Specific: "I specialize in assisting people in the fitness industry to market their business online."

Grandiose and absolute: "You *always* say you're going to get back with me and then I never hear from you."

Specific: "You said you would get back to me by Thursday with the results of your conversation with J.B. I *request* that you recommit to being in communication with me as you say you will."

You will find that when you speak with specificity results will happen much more quickly and easily. Be specific and your networking conversations will be clear, easy, and productive.

Switch from broad, vague, and grandiose to specifics

Your Mental "Search Engine"

If you notice that your automatic response to networking requests is often "I don't know anyone who ...," it may be that you are responding so quickly that you are not giving your mental computer time to access the information requested. Once you've said "I don't know," you have stopped the process of looking for the information. When you switch both your response and your thinking process, you are likely to access information that didn't immediately come to mind. A masterful networker thinks like an Internet search engine and goes exploring for information using keywords to find the resources in their mental computer.

Instead of saying "I don't know…" or "I don't have any contacts in that arena," what if you said, "I will give some thought to what you are asking for." At least you are keeping yourself open to having something come to mind that will be helpful to the person making the request. Another option is, "I know there's someone I can refer you to and I choose to recall who it is." You are then giving your brain a message to recall the information you are searching for.

There may be times when you do not have the answer or recall in that particular moment of the information that someone is asking for. If you keep saying, "I don't know," the solution/information might be there, but it may not get through to your awareness. However, when you say, "I choose to find out," or "I choose to recall," you have given your brain and your creative spirit the "go ahead" to recall the information and/or come up with a solution or resource.

Switch from "I don't know" to "I will give some thought to… ,", "I choose to recall," "I choose to find out."

"Let Me" Versus "I Will"!

Networkers who speak with authority and take responsibility for their actions create respect in their relationships. One simple way to make sure you are conveying responsibility for your actions is to upgrade the phrase "let me."

"Let me" seems like such a common, acceptable thing to say. I used to respond to questions like "Are you available to get together next week?" by saying "Let me check my calendar" or "Let me get back with you." When I switched to saying "I will check my calendar" and "I will get back with you," I noticed a feeling of greater ownership, responsibility, and self-empowerment. The phrase "let me" implies that someone else has to allow me to do the task, or give me permission to do the task, or that someone else is involved in taking the action.

In his book *Conscious Language*™, Robert Tennyson Stevens[18] suggests that we upgrade from "let me," which is in the domain of

---

18 Stevens, page 112-114.

co-dependent language to the co-empowerment language of "I will" or "I am." Doing so honors your personal power and also empowers people in your life.

Switch from "Let me" to "I will," "I am"

From Self-Sabotage to Self-Empowerment

Now that you are aware of the "self-sabotage" words you have used in the past, you have the opportunity to upgrade your "language software." I relate this whole concept of "upgrading" your words to the world of technology and how computers, cell phones, software programs, and all types of technology are constantly being upgraded. By the time I get a new laptop home and learn out how to use it, there's one on the market that's lighter weight, cheaper, faster, and has more bells and whistles. That doesn't mean that the one I bought previously wasn't good; just as the choice to upgrade your language doesn't mean you've been wrong in the past. You may have heard the expression, "when we know better, we do better." The purpose of upgrading your language is to shift into word choices that are effective, empowering, and aligned with your highest choices in life.

Some of your speaking, up until now, may have simply been cultural, habitual, or automatic. In the past you've used words and phrases that you're familiar with, without thinking about the effects on yourself and others. Speaking from habit may have been easy and comfortable; however, once you experience the results of speaking with thoughtfulness and consciousness, you will experience great ease and confidence with your conversations. Notice how you feel when you say "I request" rather than "I want." And how do you feel when you say "I choose" or "I will," rather than "I need" or "I'll try"? Notice your energy, your breath, your feelings—and choose words that bring you life-affirming energy.

Choosing New Words for New Conversations

Upgrading your "language software" provides you with new "key words," new conversations, and new networking experiences. Now that you have your language upgrades, focus on your new empowering word choices. You can't just say, "I'm not going to say *want* anymore" and create a vacuum. Instead, think about how empowered you feel when you say *choose, claim,* and *request* and focus on your new choices.

Although I am recommending that you switch-on certain words, I also remind you that this is not about any of these words being *good* or *bad* words. You are the one who gets to create your life experiences via the words you choose and the conversations you create. You now have the information and ability to consistently choose words that effectively express your heart's desire and highest choices in life.

It's Okay to Say "Oops"!

If you catch yourself saying a word or phrase that's part of your old "software program," that's okay. What's important is that you notice what you said and then use that situation as an opportunity to upgrade. There are times when I say something and immediately know there's a more clear and powerful way to communicate what I am saying. I will then either say *"oops"* or *"I choose to* restate *that"*—and *then say what I have to say with new words and new energy.* A playful attitude is helpful and can even assist you in having fun as you integrate new words into your conversations.

As you notice that you like the results of your upgrades, you will continue to speak consciously and strengthen your new, empowering choices. At some point, your shift in speaking will be so natural you won't have to think about your "new" word or phrase. Your use of empowering words in your conversations will improve your networking skills—and will also carry over into every aspect of your business and your life.

Choose Your Words Wisely and Create Conscious Conversations

Here are some examples of language upgrades for your networking interactions.

Former Habits	Language Upgrades
I *want* to have more clients	I *choose* to have more clients and will do so by ...
I *want* to grow my business	I *am* growing my business.
I *want* to get a job in	I *choose* to get a job in ...
I *want* a raise	I *request* a five percent raise
Sales are up this month	Our sales are up this month *by...*
We *have* to	We *will*
We *need* to	We *are*
Would you send me	I *request* that you send me a copy of
Let's get together for lunch sometime	I *request* we schedule a date to get together
I *don't know* how	I *will find out* how
I *don't* remember	I *choose* to recall

As a Certified Language of Mastery™ instructor, I have the privilege of providing people with information to upgrade their language and thus their lives. Along with the communication skills and networking principles I have taught for over 20 years, the language upgrades allow clients to take their conversations to a new level of connection, fulfillment, and clarity—and to achieve powerful results. You can get additional information on the topic of conscious speaking and to schedule a program for your organization, family, or team at www.DonnaFisher.com

BALANCE FOR
UPGRADING YOUR CONVERSATIONS

In this Balance you will optimize your ability to speak confidently and powerfully by choosing words that are clear, specific and empower you and others.

STEP 1. CALIBRATION: Preparing for the Process
If necessary, refer to the more detailed instructions on Calibration on page 71.

1. **Water and Hydration:** To make sure you are well hydrated, drink some water.
2. **Electrical Circuitry:** To make sure your electrical circuitry is operating efficiently, do Brain Buttons (page 61).
3. **Activating:** To make sure your body is ready to move, do The Cross Crawl (page 65).
4. **Stress Reduction:** To make sure your stress response is deactivated, do Hook-ups (page 63).
5. **Method to Use:** Select whether you will do Muscle Checking with a Partner, Self Muscle Checking, or Noticing (pages 39 to 54). (View online muscle checking demonstrations at www.SwitchedOnNetworking.com/demo.)
6. **"Yes"/"No" Response:** Use the biofeedback response method you chose to ask your body for a "yes" and then a "no" response (page 45).

NOTE: When you are in the middle of a Balance, it's possible you may begin to get inaccurate or questionable results. While this rarely occurs, it is a possibility. In case it does occur, simply repeat the Calibration procedure, and then proceed with the Balance, beginning at the point where you began to experience the inaccurate or questionable results.

STEP 2: CHECKING DONNA'S MAIN POINTS:

Read the following statements one at a time and do Muscle Checking with a Partner, Self Muscle Checking, or Noticing to determine if your body is switched-on or switched-off after saying each statement. If you are Muscle Checking with a Partner, read each statement out loud. Place a check mark next to any statements for which you are switched-off:

_____ 1. "I make clear and specific requests of others."

_____ 2. "I clearly communicate to others what I can or will do."

_____ 3. "Choosing empowering words is easy and natural for me."

_____ 4. "I am comfortable and confident making a counter offer to requests."

_____ 5. "I am comfortable asking open-ended questions to engage people in conversation."

STEP 3. IDENTIFYING TRIGGER POINTS FOR YOURSELF:

In the chart below, write down any statements from Donna's material (that aren't already listed above), that triggered an uncomfortable or negative response for you. In the right-hand column, write out your positive goal regarding the Trigger Point you identified. Muscle Check with a Partner, Self Muscle Check or Notice on both the negative side (Trigger Point) and the positive goal side of what you wrote. If you are Muscle Checking with a Partner, read the statements out loud. If you are switched off, then place a check mark by that Trigger Point. If you find that you are switched-on for the Trigger Point and positive goal statement, then what you thought was a negative Trigger Point is not one.

TRIGGER POINTS	**POSITIVE GOAL STATEMENTS**
_____	_____
_____	_____
_____	_____
_____	_____
_____	_____
_____	_____
_____	_____
_____	_____
_____	_____

If you are switched-on for all of Donna's Main Points and you did not identify any Trigger Points for yourself, then you don't have any major issues or difficulties with the information in this chapter. If this is the case, skip to Step 6 and do the Brain Gym movements and exercises listed there. By doing the Brain Gym exercises and movements even though you are already switched-on, you may achieve an even higher level of networking success.

STEP 4. ACTIONS

Now do a physical activity, role play, or visualization for at least twenty seconds for each of Donna's Main Points and for the Trigger Points you were switched-off for in Steps 2 and 3. Do Muscle Checking with a Partner, Self Muscle Checking, or Noticing for the actions as soon as you complete each one and place a check mark next to each action for which you are switched-off.

STEP 5. CHOOSING TO INCLUDE THE PAST:

Say to yourself (or out loud to your partner, if you are working with a partner): "My system now incorporates, in the most appropriate way, all relevant past events, known and unknown, into my experience." Now do Muscle Checking with a Partner, Self Muscle Checking, or Noticing for a "yes" or "no" response. (See page 45 for an explanation of a "yes" or "no" response.)

STEP 6. TAKING ACTION: Doing the Brain Gym Movements

Now's the time for you to do the Brain Gym movements listed below:
- The Cross Crawl (see page 65)
- Lazy 8s (see page 63)
- Brain Buttons (see page 61)
- Double Doodle (see page 62)
- The Thinking Cap (see page 69)
- The Owl (see page 68)
- The Calf Pump (see page 65)
- The Positive Points (see page 69)
- Hook-ups (see page 63)

STEP 7. CHECKING DONNA'S MAIN POINTS AND YOUR TRIGGER POINTS:

Now you're going to recheck the statements from Steps 2 and 3 to make sure you are switched-on for all of the Statements. If you are doing Muscle Checking with a Partner read the statements out loud, or do Self Muscle Checking, or Noticing.

1. "I make clear and specific requests of others."
2. "I clearly communicate to others what I can or will do."
3. "Choosing empowering words is easy and natural for me."
4. "I am comfortable and confident making a counter offer to requests."

5. "I am comfortable asking open-ended questions to engage people in conversation."

Repeat the Actions that you did in Step 4, doing each of them for at least twenty seconds. This time when you do the action, you will find that you are switched-on for it. It will be easier to do and you will be able to do it with less stress.

STEP 8. WHERE ARE YOU NOW?

Now that you've completed the Upgrading Your Conversations Balance, it's time to reassess your level of improvement or change from your responses to the questionnaire you originally filled out on page 96. You'll find the questions that relate to this particular Balance below.

Place a check mark in the column on the right that most clearly reflects your level of agreement or disagreement with each statement below. Then compare your current response with your initial response. Additionally, I urge you to mark your calendar and re-check your responses a month from now to assess your continued improvement. Many people find that their improvement level increases even further a month later.

		Strongly Disagree	Disagree	Doesn't Apply	Agree	Strongly Agree
14.	I speak to empower myself and others.					
15.	My requests are clear and specific, making it easy for people to respond.					
16.	I easily choose words that influence my network in a positive way.					

STEP 9. IT'S TIME TO CELEBRATE:

If you're Self Muscle Checking or Noticing, congratulate yourself. If you're working with a partner, celebrate the successful completion of the Balance for Upgrading Your Conversations and switching yourself on.

STEP 10. REINFORCING THE BALANCE WITH HOME PLAY:

Each time you finish reading and doing the Balances for the day, there's one more step before you end your Switched-On Networking session. Home play gives you the opportunity to reinforce and enhance the re-wiring and rebalancing in the brain if your mind-body feels it would be beneficial to do so. Go to Chapter 14 on page 231 and follow the directions there.

NOTE: If you are continuing to work in this current session, skip this step, and go on to the next chapter. Then, after you complete the last Balance you plan to do for the day, go to Chapter 14 and do the Home Play.

CHAPTER 12

NETWORKING AS A TIME-SAVER

Identify Statements for Balance Section:

As you read through Donna's section below, be aware of any discomfort or negativity that comes to mind about the specific suggestions she makes. Make note of these responses and, when you get to the balance, if those issues are not covered, you'll have the opportunity to write them down.

When it comes to networking, do you sometimes think, "I just don't have time to network." Or maybe your past networking experiences have garnered mixed results and you are concerned that more networking will just be another time-waster. In this chapter, we're focused on "switching-on" your thinking and your behaviors so that networking is what it is meant to be—a time saver—not a time consumer.

It's true that you can waste time online and you can waste time at networking events. You can also waste time on the phone and you can waste time sending emails. Or you can be smart, efficient, and effective with all of your networking activities, including online posting, face-to-face meetings, emails, phone calls and other activities that support you in accomplishing your desired goals.

Saving Time by Investing Time in Effective Networking

If you are not effectively networking, chances are you are spending more time than necessary playing phone tag, exchanging emails, attempting to figure things out on your own, and consuming time with unproductive and unnecessary activities. When you don't network, you end up spending more time attempting to reach people. And while you are busy doing things other than networking, you miss out on the value of the support that is available all around you.

If networking feels like a chore or it just never seems to be worthwhile in terms of results, you can feel like you are wasting your time. In fact, networking can be a waste of time:

- If you don't follow through, and create a way to stay connected with the people you meet.
- If you meet people, but never follow up with them.
- If you collect business cards and yet have no email system for staying connected.
- If you build a large database, but have nothing to offer that's of value and benefit.
- If you are scattered and don't focus on people when you are talking with them.
- If you are doing more talking than listening.
- If you are not speaking up and making requests.
- If you are hesitant to take action on the opportunities that will lead you to the fulfillment of your dreams.

Effective networking is a time saver because a strong network can assist you in accomplishing much more in less time. When you stay in touch with people, maintain contact with others, and develop strong relationships, you are more likely to get your phone calls returned quickly and easily. You also have more information available to you at your fingertips. With switched-on networking, you will find that you *actually save time by investing some time* in networking.

Successful networking does not necessarily require you to spend more time networking. Instead it is often about paying more attention to the conversations and relationships that are already part of your life. Networking is primarily about paying attention to the people around you and being truly engaged in each and every conversation so new opportunities can unfold.

I hear a lot of rumbling from people that participating in online social media sites is much too time consuming. And yet, once again, it is not about how much time you spend, but how you spend your time. Yes, it can be easy to get online, start searching around, reading everyone's posts, and find that you have spent a lot of time, with no tangible results. However, that's not the fault of the online social media site. It has more to do with having an online social media purpose and plan so that you know where to spend your time and energy to create the results you choose to create online.

The goal is to use online networking to enhance your life, not to *be* your life. It's great to use social media sites for purposes other than business. They are a great catching up with family and friends and having some relaxing "down" time from your work. Striking a balance between work and pleasure is important to your well-being.

If you have a tendency to spend "too much" time online, set some parameters and guidelines so that your online networking is time efficient. Here are some ideas to consider:

- Designate a certain time or a certain amount of time to spend on social media sites. Set a timer so that you don't lose track of time.
- Be selective about the sites, blogs, and online subscriptions that you sign up for rather than spreading yourself too thin, which can result in being ineffective on all of the sites. Choose those sites that are high-quality and directly related to your business, passions, and/or topics you are interested in learning.
- Check out the features that allow your postings on one site to automatically post on your other online sites.
- Create online connections with people whose postings will likely be of value and interest to you.
- Make sure your email system is set so that emails that are not important to you are automatically placed in a "junk" file or "spam" file.

Effective networking is the smart approach to connecting with people and passing along information. Building good relationships makes good business sense. People who have achieved success can tell you there are a lot of people who helped them along the way. Rather than thinking of networking as something to do, think of it as a way of being and relating to people. Networking is not a technique used to get people to do what you want. Networking is living a lifestyle of connections and service.

Rather than having to do and learn everything on your own, your network allows you to leverage your actions and ideas. By leveraging your resources you attain greater results in a shorter amount of time and/or with less effort.

Be a One-Minute Networker

Networking happens in that moment when you share a valuable piece of information with someone or someone passes along beneficial information to you. A "networking moment" can happen with someone you just met or someone who has been a lifelong friend.

Rather than thinking of networking as something that takes a lot of time, think of networking as something that can happen at any moment, in any conversation, as long as you are paying attention to the opportunity. Networking consists of many little things you can do to have networking be a time saver and opportunity creator in your life. Here are some fast, simple, and easy behaviors for creating valuable connections. It only takes a minute to:

- Say thanks
- Ask for help
- Give a referral
- Write a thank you note
- Initiate a conversation
- Say something encouraging
- Introduce yourself
- Respond to an e-mail
- Offer support
- Provide a new insight or idea
- Post a message online
- Forward information that could be of interest and value to someone else

Live a life of "one-minute behaviors" that make a difference! Discover how easy, fun and rewarding networking can be. Over the long term, the effect of even just one phone call a day will be significant in achieving a vibrant and active network. The cumulative effect of networking can enrich your life in many ways. Remember, it only takes a minute.

How Does Effective Networking Save Time?

When you switch-on your networking skills,
you will find that life is easier and more fun because:

- People tend to return your phone calls more promptly because they already feel connected with you and are interested in what you are doing.

- You have quicker, easier access to people, information, and ideas because you have people in your network who can (and will) link you to people in their network.

- You don't have to reinvent the wheel because you are comfortable and effective asking for support and information from people who have the experience and expertise that moves your project forward more quickly.

- You can generate results from the people right around you because you generate interesting conversations and respond to people and opportunities all around you.

- You can significantly reduce the time it takes to do research on a topic or issue because someone you know will know someone who has the information that relates to your project.

- You can reach a multitude of people with one posting, invitation, or promotion through one of the online programs/services.

- You can reinforce and enhance "your brand" easily and economically through the messages that you post online that will be seen by people around the world and passed along to people you don't even know.

- You can get feedback from customers, prospects, peers through online surveys that are quick and easy to set up, send, and tabulate.

- When you are looking for a resource, you will typically already have someone in your network who offers that particular product or service so you don't have to search around. Your contact is at your fingertips.

- You can get information by simply starting a discussion group online or posting questions for people to respond with the desired information.

Consistent Actions Create Efficiency

Everyone has a vast and powerful network. Yet your own personal network may become ineffective and dormant at times because you get busy, distracted, or simply forget to continually stay connected with your network. Without action and attention, your network is like a field of grain that never gets harvested. Your network consists of a wealth of information, ideas, and contacts that can be of tremendous value to yourself and others. To harvest your network requires taking appropriate action to access information and pass it along to the right people in a timely and professional manner.

Consistent, productive actions over time lead to great efficiency. Consistency leads to the development of productive habits. And once something becomes a habit it happens easily, automatically, and with little effort. Over time these action steps will become the habits that lead to a networking lifestyle that creates more and more results with less time and effort:

- **Introduce people to one another.** When you connect the people in your network with each other you are strengthening your overall network.
- **Introduce yourself to new people.** Meeting new people creates connections that lead to new opportunities.
- **Make requests.** Ask for information, names, ideas, support, encouragement, and recommendations.
- **Send notes.** Sending cards, letters, emails, and online messages helps you stay in touch with people and keeps your networking links alive and active. It is also a way of nurturing the "seed" that you have planted so that the relationship can grow into more networking opportunities.
- **Attend community, professional and networking events—both online and face-to-face.** Step up and show up. Be engaged in what's going on in your community and industry.
- **Exchange business cards and provide contact information.** Make the exchange of business cards a natural part of your conversations. On your social media sites, complete your profile with your photo and contact information so that people have an easy way to get to know you.

- **Give information, contacts, and referrals.** Be proactive and look for ways to give and share the information that you have with others. Recommend products and services that have been beneficial for you.
- **Respond to people's requests.** Listen to what people are saying and pay attention when they make a request so that you can tap into your network of resources to help them make a powerful connection.
- **Create an online presence.** Make good use of your time on the internet to connect with people, find career opportunities, create visibility for your business, and strengthen your brand.
- **Take the time to learn about other people's businesses and goals.** Share your expertise when what you have learned can be helpful to others. Be available to brainstorm to come up with new, innovative ideas.
- **Post online messages consistently.** By being consistent with your postings you build your brand, while also offering valuable information to your online network.

Integrate Networking into Your Life

Effective networking is more about the quality of your actions and interactions than it is about the amount of time you spend networking. You save time with networking when you integrate it seamlessly into your life so you are paying attention in each conversation and connecting with people in your everyday situations. Networking becomes the natural way you listen, interact, and respond to people and opportunities. Integrating networking into your lifestyle involves:

- Paying attention to each conversation.
- Really listening to what people are saying.
- Responding to people's postings, phone calls, and emails.
- In each conversation, ask, offer, and thank people.

BALANCE FOR NETWORKING AS A TIME-SAVER

In this Balance you will optimize your ability to use your time efficiently, effectively, and wisely when networking.

STEP 1. CALIBRATION: Preparing for the Process
> If necessary, refer to the more detailed instructions on Calibration on page 71.
>
> 1. **Water and Hydration:** To make sure you are well hydrated, drink some water.
> 2. **Electrical Circuitry:** To make sure your electrical circuitry is operating efficiently, do Brain Buttons (page 61).
> 3. **Activating:** To make sure your body is ready to move, do The Cross Crawl (page 65).
> 4. **Stress Reduction:** To make sure your stress response is deactivated, do Hook-ups (page 63).
> 5. **Method to Use:** Select whether you will do Muscle Checking with a Partner, Self Muscle Checking, or Noticing (pages 39 to 54). (View online muscle checking demonstrations at www.SwitchedOnNetworking.com/demo.)
> 6. **"Yes"/"No" Response:** Use the biofeedback response method you chose to ask your body for a "yes" and then a "no" response (page 45).

NOTE: When you are in the middle of a Balance, it's possible you may begin to get inaccurate or questionable results. While this rarely occurs, it is a possibility. In case it does occur, simply repeat the Calibration procedure, and then proceed with the Balance, beginning at the point where you began to experience the inaccurate or questionable results.

STEP 2: CHECKING DONNA'S MAIN POINTS:
> Read the following statements one at a time and do Muscle Checking with a Partner, Self Muscle Checking, or Noticing

to determine if your body is switched-on or switched-off after saying each statement. If you are Muscle Checking with a Partner, read each statement out loud. Place a check mark next to any statements for which you are switched-off:

_____ 1. "I connect with people in a way that respects their time."

_____ 2. "I network efficiently and effectively."

_____ 3. "I use my time and resources wisely when I am networking."

_____ 4. "I take time to connect with people."

_____ 5. "I allow my network to help me accomplish my goals quickly and easily."

STEP 3. IDENTIFYING TRIGGER POINTS FOR YOURSELF:

In the chart below, write down any statements from Donna's material (that aren't already listed above), that triggered an uncomfortable or negative response for you. In the right-hand column, write out your positive goal regarding the Trigger Point you identified. Muscle Check with a Partner, Self Muscle Check or Notice on both the negative side (Trigger Point) and the positive goal side of what you wrote. If you are Muscle Checking with a Partner, read the statements out loud. If you are switched off, then place a check mark by that Trigger Point. If you find that you are switched-on for the Trigger Point and positive goal statement, then what you thought was a negative Trigger Point is not one.

TRIGGER POINTS	POSITIVE GOAL STATEMENTS
_____	_____
_____	_____
_____	_____
_____	_____

_____   _____
_____   _____
_____   _____
_____   _____
_____   _____
_____   _____

If you are switched-on for all of Donna's Main Points and you did not identify any Trigger Points for yourself, then you don't have any major issues or difficulties with the information in this chapter. If this is the case, skip to Step 6 and do the Brain Gym movements and exercises listed there. By doing the Brain Gym exercises and movements even though you are already switched-on, you may achieve an even higher level of networking success.

STEP 4. ACTIONS:

Now do a physical activity, role play, or visualization for at least twenty seconds for each of Donna's Main Points and for the Trigger Points you were switched-off for in Steps 2 and 3. Do Muscle Checking with a Partner, Self Muscle Checking, or Noticing for the actions as soon as you complete each one and place a check mark next to each action for which you are switched-off.

STEP 5. CHOOSING TO INCLUDE THE PAST:

Say to yourself (or out loud to your partner, if you are working with a partner): "My system now incorporates, in the most appropriate way, all relevant past events, known and unknown, into my experience." Now do Muscle Checking with a Partner, Self Muscle Checking, or Noticing for a "yes" or "no" response. (See page 45 for an explanation of a "yes" or "no" response.)

STEP 6. TAKING ACTION: Doing the Brain Gym Movements

Now's the time for you to do the Brain Gym movements listed below. (See the instructions and illustrations for each of the Brain Gym movements in Chapter 4 beginning on page 57.)

- The Cross Crawl (see page 65)
- Lazy 8s (see page 63)
- Brain Buttons (see page 61)
- Earth Buttons (see page 62)
- Space Buttons (see page 64)
- Balance Buttons (see page 60)
- The Thinking Cap (see page 69)
- The Footflex (see page 67)
- The Owl (see page 68)

STEP 7. CHECKING DONNA'S MAIN POINTS AND YOUR TRIGGER POINTS:

Now you're going to recheck the statements from Steps 2 and 3 to make sure you are switched-on for all of the Statements. If you are doing Muscle Checking with a Partner read the statements out loud, or do Self Muscle Checking, or Noticing.

1. "I connect with people in a way that respects their time."
2. "I network efficiently and effectively."
3. "I use my time and resources wisely when I am networking."
4. "I take time to connect with people."
5. "I allow my network to help me accomplish my goals quickly and easily."

Repeat the Actions that you did in Step 4, doing each of them for at least twenty seconds. This time when you do the action, you will find that you are switched-on for it. It will be easier to do and you will be able to do it with less stress.

STEP 8. WHERE ARE YOU NOW?

Now that you've completed the Balance for Networking as a Time-Saver, it's time to reassess your level of improvement or change from your responses to the questionnaire on page 96. You'll find the questions that relate to this particular Balance below.

Place a check mark in the column on the right that most clearly reflects your level of agreement or disagreement with each statement below. Then compare your current response with your initial response. Additionally, I urge you to mark your calendar and re-check your responses a month from now to assess your continued improvement. Many people find that their improvement level increases even more a month later.

		Strongly Disagree	Disagree	Doesn't Apply	Agree	Strongly Agree
17.	I network efficiently, saving myself time and energy.					
18.	I am effective as a result of having a strong network of support.					

STEP 9. IT'S TIME TO CELEBRATE:

If you're Self Muscle Checking or Noticing, congratulate yourself. If you're working with a partner, celebrate the successful completion of the Balance for Networking as a Time-Saver and switching yourself on.

STEP 10. REINFORCING THE BALANCE WITH HOME PLAY:

Each time you finish reading and doing the Balances for the day, there's one more step before you end your Switched-On Networking session. Home play gives you the opportunity to reinforce and enhance the re-wiring and rebalancing in the brain if your mind-body feels it would be beneficial to do so. Go to Chapter 14 on page 231 and follow the directions there.

NOTE: If you are continuing to work in this current session, skip this step, and go on to the next chapter. Then, after you complete the last Balance you plan to do for the day, go to Chapter 14 and do the Home Play.

CHAPTER 13

BEING A PROSPEROUS NETWORKER

Identify Statements for Balance Section:

As you read through Donna's section below, be aware of any discomfort or negativity that comes to mind about the specific suggestions she makes. Make note of these responses and, when you get to the balance, if those issues are not covered, you'll have the opportunity to write them down.

Do you consider yourself to be rich because you have a wealth of friends you can call on and count on? Or do you consider yourself to be rich when you have a large balance on your bank statements and investment portfolios? Or maybe you experience being rich as a combination of having both intrinsic and material wealth. Being rich, prosperous, and profitable can be experienced in many different ways. It's all based on your definition and your perspective.

One of the great things about networking is that it can contribute to your experience of "richness" in all areas of your life—if you so choose. For you to fully experience that richness however, you must have the mindset to be willing to receive and to feel the richness that life offers you.

A master networker understands the big picture and enjoys rich rewards. I've talked about how networking is about giving, contributing, being there for people. And yet, that's only one side of the networking process. Networking is a two-way street. Your own sense of worth is instrumental in allowing you to accept the respect, admiration, and richness of your network.

If I don't allow others to contribute to me, I actually block my networking relationships from deepening because I end up shutting people out. If I don't have a sense of being able to handle wealth, I may find big opportunities too scary to follow through on. If I believe that resources and money is scarce, then I limit myself from taking the actions that can lead to new resources and financial income.

Jerry's Brain Gym balance in this chapter will rewire your subconscious beliefs about prosperity so that you can receive all that your network has to offer. It's not enough to "want" money, wealth, and financial success. As we talked about in Chapter 11, Upgrading Your Conversations, the definition of the word "want" is actually "to lack." Having prosperity is about having the "right" mindset *and* taking the "right" action steps. Rather than focusing on what appears to be lacking in your life, think about the vastness of your network and how your network is rich with resources—everything you could imagine—and more! Your network can be your mental reminder that you have an abundance of resources available to you. If you start to think "scarcity," switch your thinking and begin to explore the vastness of your network.

Prosperity and success can be defined in many different ways; each individual must define it in their own way. You choose what living a rich life means to you. To fully embrace all that your network has to offer requires that you be open to receiving, to being successful and to experiencing a rich, vastly rewarding life.

Oftentimes people expect networking to be their get rich quick magical potion before they develop their mental capacity for wealth. But networking is not a get rich quick scheme. Networking is about taking steps—large or small—to make your dreams come true in whatever way you define your dreams. There are really no limits to the heights you can attain when you switch-on your prosperity quotient.

The definition of "prosperity" and "prosperous" includes "flourishing, rich, affluent, wealth, promising and of good fortune." Create a prosperous network—one that is flourishing, rich with resources, promising of results and providing good fortune for yourself and others.

When Your Networking is "Unconditional" Surprising Doors Open

Even those who have a well-developed networking plan never know where great opportunities will show up. My suggestion is to focus less on the obvious and lean into the "unconditional." When your networking is "unconditional," you are connecting with people and sharing resources without conditions—giving to be giving, serving to be serving, connecting to be connecting. You may be surprised by the doors that will open for you when you approach your daily life, both within your profession and in every other arena of life, as an opportunity to simply and graciously "connect." Any conversation you have could lead to something very important for your success.

A friend of mine developed one of those "unconditional" networking connections simply by reaching out to a stranger at church. It's part of Rich's personality to mingle and talk with people in the church courtyard after the Sunday morning service. And it's not uncommon for him to seek out and approach some of the people who appear to be a bit shy or quiet or off by themselves. In doing so, one day Rich struck up a conversation with a man who had recently started attending church in his desire to turn his life around.

Every Sunday Rich would say hi and visit with this man for a little bit. Each time he would get to know him a little more. Eventually, the man shared with Rich that he had reached six months of sobriety and that it was especially important to him at this time in his life to have support towards his recovery and his commitment to create a good life for himself.

Rich offered his support by inviting the man to call him every week just to let him know how he was doing and to call anytime that he might just be looking for someone to talk with. The friendship grew to the point to where they would occasionally meet for breakfast. Rich knew the man didn't have a car and rode the bus to work. He also noticed the he was always courteous and professional. The man was appreciative and even sent Rich a note thanking him for his friendship and support.

Then one day, out of the blue, the man told Rich, who happened to be a stockbroker, that he had received a six-figure inheritance from relatives. Although he had a broker at one time in the past, the guy treated him so shabbily that he had gotten frustrated and was now looking elsewhere for assistance. He wanted to know if Rich would be his broker.

Rich said he never even had a thought that befriending this man would lead to business. His offer of friendship and support was never about anything other than being there for someone else. He would never in his wildest dreams have imagined that this man would become one of his clients. And yet, that's what happened.

Rich says it never would have mattered if the man had never given anything back to him, because he benefited emotionally from reaching out and giving and extending his friendship and support. Rich reached out without judgment or expectations, knowing that everyone experiences life's ups and downs and that friendship and support is what's most important when any of us is going through challenges.

The two men's friendship and professional relationship has stayed in track for some time now. Rich took his friend on a ride in his plane. And the man is now teaching art to children at the church and is blossoming in many ways, personally, spiritually, and professionally. Just like everyone, he still has those tough days and Rich is pleased to know that he is still considered the kind of friend and confidant that the man can call on those days just to talk.

Another interesting part of this story is that Rich had previously met another man in the courtyard who turned out to be a "taker." He was always asking for money, showed up at Rich's office unannounced and acted inappropriately, and was unappreciative and abusive of the friendship. One of the things I greatly appreciate about Rich's story is that he did not let his experience with the "taker" jade his view of people. He did not color the world with his experience and decide to stop reaching out to connect and contribute. Rich's attitude is that you keep going till you find people you can be of value to. Rich's closing comments in sharing this story with me was, "You never know."

BALANCE FOR BEING A PROSPEROUS NETWORKER

In this Balance, you will re-educate your brain to release blockages and create prosperity and financial success for yourself.

STEP 1. CALIBRATION: Preparing for the Process

If necessary, refer to the more detailed instructions on Calibration on page 71.

1. **Water and Hydration:** To make sure you are well hydrated, drink some water.

2. **Electrical Circuitry:** To make sure your electrical circuitry is operating efficiently, do Brain Buttons (page 61).

3. **Activating:** To make sure your body is ready to move, do The Cross Crawl (page 65).

4. **Stress Reduction:** To make sure your stress response is deactivated, do Hook-ups (page 63).

5. **Method to Use:** Select whether you will do Muscle Checking with a Partner, Self Muscle Checking, or Noticing (pages 39 to 54). (View online muscle checking demonstrations at www.SwitchedOnNetworking.com/demo.)

6. **"Yes"/"No" Response:** Use the biofeedback response method you chose to ask your body for a "yes" and then a "no" response (page 45).

NOTE: When you are in the middle of a Balance, it's possible you may begin to get inaccurate or questionable results. While this rarely occurs, it is a possibility. In case it does occur, simply repeat the Calibration procedure, and then proceed with the Balance, beginning at the point where you began to experience the inaccurate or questionable results.

STEP 2: CHECKING DONNA'S MAIN POINTS:

Read the following statements one at a time and do Muscle Checking with a Partner, Self Muscle Checking, or Noticing to determine if your body is switched-on or switched-off after saying each statement. If you are Muscle Checking with a Partner, read each statement out loud. Place a check mark next to any statements for which you are switched-off:

_____ 1. "I bring a prosperity consciousness to my networking interactions."

_____ 2. "I am worthy of the admiration, trust, and respect of the people in my network."

_____ 3. "I am willing for my networking activities to pay off abundantly."

_____ 4. "I network with the intention of having myself and others reap rich rewards in life."

_____ 5. "I appreciate and accept the abundance that my network provides to me."

STEP 3. IDENTIFYING TRIGGER POINTS FOR YOURSELF:

In the chart below, write down any statements from Donna's material (that aren't already listed above), that triggered an uncomfortable or negative response for you. In the right-hand column, write out your positive goal regarding the Trigger Point you identified. Muscle Check with a Partner, Self Muscle Check or Notice on both the negative side (Trigger Point) and the positive goal side of what you wrote. If you are Muscle Checking with a Partner, read the statements out loud. If you are switched off, then place a check mark by that Trigger Point. If you find that you are switched-on for the Trigger Point and positive goal statement, then what you thought was a negative Trigger Point is not one.

TRIGGER POINTS	POSITIVE GOAL STATEMENTS
_____	_____
_____	_____
_____	_____
_____	_____
_____	_____
_____	_____
_____	_____
_____	_____
_____	_____

If you are switched-on for all of Donna's Main Points and you did not identify any Trigger Points for yourself, then you don't have any major issues or difficulties with the information in this chapter. If this is the case, skip to Step 6 and do the Brain Gym movements and exercises listed there. By doing the Brain Gym exercises and movements even though you are already switched-on, you may achieve an even higher level of networking success.

STEP 4. ACTIONS:

Now do a physical activity, role play, or visualization for at least twenty seconds for each of Donna's Main Points and for the Trigger Points you were switched-off for in Steps 2 and 3. Do Muscle Checking with a Partner, Self Muscle Checking, or Noticing for the actions as soon as you complete each one and place a check mark next to each action for which you are switched-off.

STEP 5. CHOOSING TO INCLUDE THE PAST:

Say to yourself (or out loud to your partner, if you are working with a partner): "My system now incorporates, in the most appropriate way, all relevant past events, known and unknown, into my experience." Now do Muscle Checking with a Partner, Self Muscle Checking, or Noticing for a "yes" or "no" response. (See page 45 for an explanation of a "yes" or "no" response.)

STEP 6. TAKING ACTION: Doing the Brain Gym Movements

Do the Brain Gym Movements listed below:

- The Cross Crawl (see page 65)
- Lazy 8s (see page 63)
- Brain Buttons (see page 61)
- The Thinking Cap (see page 69)
- Hook-ups (see page 63)
- The Positive Points (see page 69)
- Arm Activation (see page 60)
- Space Buttons (see page 64)
- The Grounder (see page 67)

STEP 7. CHECKING DONNA'S MAIN POINTS AND YOUR TRIGGER POINTS:

Now you're going to recheck the statements from Steps 2 and 3 to make sure you are switched-on for all of the Statements. If you are doing Muscle Checking with a Partner read the statements out loud, or do Self Muscle Checking, or Noticing.

1. "I bring a prosperity consciousness to my networking interactions."
2. "I am worthy of the admiration, trust, and respect of the people in my network."
3. "I am willing for my networking activities to pay off abundantly."
4. "I network with the intention of having myself and others reap rich rewards in life."
5. "I appreciate and accept the abundance that my network provides to me."

Repeat the Actions that you did in Step 4, doing each of them for at least twenty seconds. This time when you do the action, you will find that you are switched-on for it. It will be easier to do and you will be able to do it with less stress.

STEP 8. WHERE ARE YOU NOW?

Now that you've completed the Balance for Being a Prosperous Networker, it's time to reassess your level of improvement or change from your responses to the questionnaire on page 96. You'll find the questions that relate to this particular Balance below.

Place a check mark in the column on the right that most clearly reflects your level of agreement or disagreement with each statement below. Then compare your current response with your initial response. Additionally, I urge you to mark your calendar and re-check your responses a month from now to assess your continued improvement. Many people find that their improvement level increases even more a month later.

		Strongly Disagree	Disagree	Doesn't Apply	Agree	Strongly Agree
19.	My prosperity consciousness enhances my joy in sharing ideas and information with my network.					
20.	My network is a source of abundance in all areas of my life.					

STEP 9. IT'S TIME TO CELEBRATE:

If you're Self Muscle Checking or Noticing, congratulate yourself. If you're working with a partner, celebrate the successful completion of the Balance for Being a Prosperous Networker and switching yourself on.

STEP 10. REINFORCING THE BALANCE WITH HOME PLAY:

Each time you finish reading and doing the Balances for the day, there's one more step before you end your Switched-On Networking session. Home play gives you the opportunity to reinforce and enhance the re-wiring and rebalancing in the brain if your mind-body feels it would be beneficial to do so. Go to Chapter 14 on page 231 and follow the directions there.

NOTE: If you are continuing to work in this current session, skip this step, and go on to the next chapter. Then, after you complete the last Balance you plan to do for the day, go to Chapter 14 and do the Home Play.

PART III

REINFORCEMENT

BY JERRY V. TEPLITZ, J.D., PH.D.

CHAPTER 14

Reinforcing with Home Play

Home Play is a series of Brain Gym movements that will reinforce and enhance the re-wiring and balancing that you did in the Balances. As we covered earlier, when you do the Balances, you are creating new neural pathways among the various parts of the brain, including the left and right hemispheres and the corpus callosum, which is the connective tissue in the center of the brain that connects the two hemispheres. You might think of it this way: It's as if you are creating a new highway where previously none existed. When you add the reinforcement, you are turning the highway into a superhighway. That further strengthens and enhances the new pathways that have been created.

First, you will determine if the body needs to do Home Play. If your body indicates that it doesn't need to do any Home Play, that's fine. If that's the case, you'll get a "no" response in Step 1 below and then you'll stop this process. This means you did all the re-wiring and balancing that needed to be done. It's as if you baked a cake and iced it and got to eat it, too!

If you get a "yes" response, you will determine which of the Brain Gym Movements your body wants to do to fully reinforce and integrate the Brain Gym Balances in Switched-On Networking at a deeper level. Then you will ask the body how many times a day and for how many days it wants to do the movements and exercises that it has chosen as reinforcement.

BRAIN GYM HOME PLAY
SELECTION PROCESS

STEP 1. DECIDING IF YOU NEED TO DO HOME PLAY:

If you are Muscle Checking with a Partner, read the following statement to your partner and muscle check. If you are Noticing or Self Muscle Checking, read it out loud to yourself and check: "This system wants to do the Brain Gym movements and exercises to reinforce the Balances in the *Switched-On Networking* book." Do Muscle Checking with a Partner, Self Muscle Checking, or Noticing.

If you get a "yes" response, go on to Step 2. If you get a "no," stop. This means your body doesn't need to do any reinforcement. It means your body feels the learning in the Balances is complete.

Step 2. CREATING THE LIST:

If "yes," say out loud to yourself (or to your partner, if you are working with a partner): "This body wants to do the following movements."

Then read the list of Brain Gym movements listed below. Do Muscle Checking with a Partner, Self Muscle Checking, or Noticing after saying each movement name, then record the names of those you get a "yes" response to on the blank lines below the list. You are not actually going to be doing the movements and exercises right now; you are just creating your reinforcement list.

Alphabet 8s	Earth Buttons	The Elephant
Arm Activation	Hook-ups	The Footflex
Balance Buttons	Lazy 8s	The Grounder
Belly Breathing	Space Buttons	The Owl
Brain Buttons	The Calf Pump	The Positive Points
Double Doodle	The Cross Crawl	The Thinking Cap

Your List:

_____	_____
_____	_____
_____	_____
_____	_____
_____	_____
_____	_____
_____	_____
_____	_____

STEP 3. CONFIRMATION ON NUMBER OF DAYS

Say out loud to yourself (or to your partner, if you are working with a partner): "This body wants to do these movements at least once a day… at least twice a day… at least three times a day… at least four times a day…" etc. Do Muscle Checking with a Partner, Self Muscle Checking, or Noticing for each one.

If you get a "yes" response on once a day, check again to see if you should do the movements twice a day. Continue checking until you get a "no" response. For example, if you get a "no" when you check three times a day, that means your last "yes" was two times a day, so you will do the movements twice a day.

STEP 4. CONFIRMATION ON NUMBER OF WEEKS

Say out loud to yourself (or to your partner, if you are working with a partner): "This body wants to do these movements for at least one week… at least two weeks… at least three weeks…" etc. Do Muscle Checking with a Partner, Self Muscle Checking or Noticing for each one.

Let's say you get a "yes" response on one week. Next, you'll check if you should do them for two weeks. Continue checking until you get a "no" response. For example, if you get a "no" response when you check three times a week, this means your last "yes" was two weeks, so you will do the movements for two weeks.

SUMMARY: At the end of this process, you will have selected a specific group of Brain Gym movements to do for a certain number of repetitions per day, for a specific number of weeks. Now enjoy your reinforcement.

CHAPTER 15

THE SEVEN-MINUTE TUNE UP: REINFORCING BRAIN GYM ON AN EVERYDAY BASIS

The purpose of the Seven-Minute Tune Up is to begin every day on a positive note. It's a way to bring focus, concentration, balance, and energy to your brain and your body. I suggest doing the Seven-Minute Tune Up the first thing every day. You can also do it during the day if something negative happens or if you need to re-energize or refocus during your day.

1. **WATER**
   Drink a glass of water.

2. **BREATHE FOR RELAXATION**
   Inhale through the nose while touching the tip of the tongue to the roof of the mouth just behind the teeth. Then drop the tongue and exhale through the mouth. Do this for four to six complete breaths. As an alternative, you can do the Belly Breathing on page 61.

3. **BRAIN BUTTONS**
   Place one hand on your belly button. With the thumb and fingers of the other hand locate the two hollow areas below the collarbone. The hollows are one or two inches away from the sternum, which is the bone that runs down the center of the chest. Rub these areas vigorously for thirty seconds.

4. HOOK-UPS

This movement is done in two parts:

PART I

Sit in a chair or stand, clasp your hands together. Whichever thumb is on top will be considered your primary side. Release your hands and extend your hands in front of you with the back of each hand facing the other. Cross the primary side hand over the top of the other hand, intertwine your fingers. Draw your hands under and into your chest.

Cross your primary side ankle in front of the other ankle. Place your tongue against the roof of your mouth, one quarter inch behind your front teeth. Keep breathing through your nose. Hold for thirty seconds.

PART II

Uncross your legs. Place the fingertips of both of your hands together, forming a teepee. Keep your eyes closed, the tongue up, and continue to breathe. Hold for thirty seconds.

5. THE POSITIVE POINTS

Just above the center of the eyebrows, and halfway up to the hairline you will find a slight bump where the head curves. Place three fingers together lightly on the bumps. Close your eyes and breathe.

Hold the points for thirty seconds to one minute.

6. THE CROSS CRAWL

To do The Cross Crawl "march in place," lifting the knees high. At the same time, reach across and touch the knees—or somewhere on the leg—with the opposite hands. Continue for thirty seconds.

Variations of The Cross Crawl:

There are other ways to achieve the effect of The Cross Crawl. You might want to experience each of them. This will vary the way you do The Cross Crawl:

- Instead of touching your hands to the opposite legs, go all the way down and touch the heels. Continue by alternating touching opposite hands to the heels.
- Use your elbows instead of your hands to touch the knees. Continue by alternating touching opposite elbows to the knees. This variation of The Cross Crawl stretches the core stomach muscles.
- Touch your left heel behind you with your right hand, being sure to keep the left hand to the front. Continue by alternating touching opposite hands and heels to the back.

APPENDIX A

CALIBRATION PROCEDURE – COMPREHENSIVE METHOD

In Chapter 5 you learned a fast, easy method of Calibration, the process that is used at the beginning of any Balance. As an option, those who are more experienced in the use of Muscle Checking as a biofeedback response system may choose to do this more comprehensive method of Calibration. To do this method you will need to work with a partner.

PART 1. NEUTRAL:

    With your partner, do Muscle Checking with a Partner for Normal response, which you learned earlier in Chapter 3 (see page 39). It's important to do this step so you get the feel for your partner's level of resistance. It's also an opportunity for the Checkee to give you feedback so you can determine if the pressure is too hard for his arm.

PART 2. NEED FOR WATER:

    The second part of Calibration is to determine if the body is hydrated or dehydrated. In this comprehensive method of Calibration, the procedure used to check if the body is adequately hydrated is an adaptation of a method used by veterinarians to check for dehydration in animals. Vets check the elasticity of the animal's skin by grabbing hold of the skin on the back of the neck, which is called the scruff, and pulling gently or pinching it together and then releasing it. If the animal's body has enough water, the skin quickly springs back to its normal position; however, if the animal needs water, the skin is slow to return to normal. This same test can be used with people to determine the level of dehydration by pulling up on the skin for a few seconds and then releasing it. If the skin doesn't immediately return to its original state, the person is dehydrated.

In Brain Gym, we use a similar method, but one that doesn't require you to pinch or pull your partner's skin. Instead, the person being checked pulls a small clump of his own hair and says **"Pusssshhhhh"** while he is being muscle checked. If his arm stays up, it means he has enough water and is hydrated. If it goes down, either he needs water or the person doing the muscle checking needs water. Therefore, if the arm does go down, the correction is for both of you to drink some water. Then repeat this muscle check by having your partner again pull his hair. Now his arm should easily stay up. Because some water molecules are absorbed in the mouth, it takes the body only a fifth of a second to register the fact that you have had a drink of water.

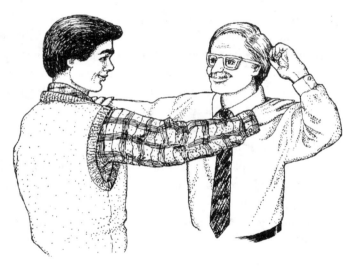

If his arm is switched-off, both of you should drink some water and then repeat this muscle checking procedure. If the arm is still switched-off, both of you should take another sip of water and check again. Continue this procedure until the arm is switched-on.

PART 3. ELECTRICAL CIRCUITRY:

Checking the electrical circuitry confirms that regardless of which hand you use to perform the muscle checking on your partner, you will get accurate answers. In essence what we're doing here is calibrating to make sure the person's body will give appropriate responses, no matter which hand is used to do the checking. If the person's arm goes down when you check electrical circuitry, the Brain Gym movement called Brain Buttons (page 61) is done as a correction.

For Muscle Checking with a Partner do steps below:

1. Place one hand on your partner's extended arm above the wrist bone and ask your partner to say "Pussss hhhh" as you do the muscle check.

2. Place your other hand on your partner's arm above the wrist bone and ask your partner to say "Pusssshhhhh" as you do the muscle check.

3. Once again, place your first hand on your partner's arm and ask your partner to say "Pusssshhhhh" as you do the muscle check.

On Steps 1, 2, and 3 your partner's arm should remain switched-on. If your partner's arm is switched-off on any of these three steps, stop here and both do Brain Buttons (see page 61). Then repeat Part 3 again. Your partner should now be switched-on for all three checks.

PART 4. ACTIVATING:

In this part of calibration, you are switching your system into gear to do the physical movements Brain Gym requires. You are activating your body to move. If the person's arm is switched-off on this step, the correction is doing 30 seconds of The Cross Crawl (page 65) and then re-checking to be sure the person is now switched-on for activity.

For Muscle Checking with a Partner do the steps below:

1. Ask your partner to use one of his fingers to find the bottom rib of his right rib cage at the place

where it comes to a point. This point is located almost in line with the arm pit.

2. Then ask him to move his finger straight up from that spot about two inches. This is where the Activating point is located and where you will be checking him.

3. Now have him release this point and you place one of your fingers at this point. Ask your partner to say "Pussssh" as you do the muscle check on your partner. His arm should be switched-on.

If your partner's arm is switched-off on this step, stop here and both of you should do The Cross Crawl on page 65 for thirty seconds. Then repeat Step 3 again. Your partner should now be switched-on for this check.

PART 5. STRESS REDUCTION:

In the Stress Reduction steps we muscle check the Central Meridian Line (based on acupuncture concepts), which runs from the belly button area to the area below the lower lip. If the person gives an inappropriate response to this muscle check—for example, the arm stayed up when it should have come down—it means that she is over-energized. I have added an additional method of Correction for Individuals Showing an Over-Energy Response that I believe is faster than Hook-ups and works most of the time. The instructions for both methods are below.

For Muscle Checking with a Partner do steps below:

1. "Zip Up" by tracing a line with your hand from your partner's belly button to his nose. Ask your partner to say "Pusssshhhhh"

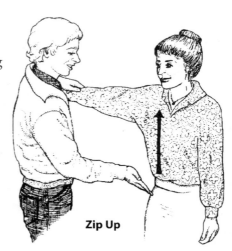

Zip Up

and do the muscle check. Your partner's arm should remain switched-on.

2. "Zip Down" by tracing a line with your hand from your partner's nose to his belly button. Ask your partner to say "Pusssshhhhh" and do the muscle check. Your partner's arm should be switched-off.

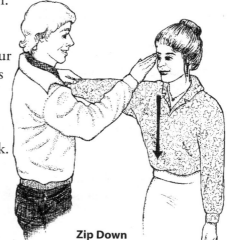

Zip Down

3. "Zip Up" again by tracing a line with your hand from your partner's belly button to his nose without touching his body. Ask your partner to say "Pusssshhhhh" and do the muscle check. Your partner's arm should remain switched-on once again.

If your partner's arm gave an inconsistent response on the muscle checking for the "Zip Up" (it came down when it was supposed to stay up) or "Zip Down" (it stayed up when it was supposed to come down), then you should stop here and both of you do the Correction for Individuals Showing an Over-Energy Response, which is below. Then repeat Steps 1, 2 and 3 again. Your partner's muscle checking responses will most likely be appropriate now. If they are not appropriate, both of you should do the Brain Gym movement Hook-ups on page 63. Then repeat the muscle checking and it should be appropriate.

CORRECTIONS FOR INDIVIDUALS SHOWING AN OVER-ENERGY RESPONSE

One of the Corrections for Individuals Showing an Over-Energy Response is to do Hook-ups (see page 63).

The second Correction method used in Switched-On Networking works most of the time. This method was developed by Roger Callahan, Ph.D. and is taught in his book *Tapping the Healer Within.*

Ask the person to tap the fleshy part of the side of one hand, located just below the pinkie finger, against the same area on the other hand. This is the part of the hand that you would use to give a karate chop. She should do this 35 to 45 times.

This simple activity seems to turn off the person's overactive adrenal glands for at least a short period of time, allowing you to get accurate muscle checking results. This tapping method works most of the time; however, if the muscle checking responses still do not match what the pattern should be in Part 5, have the person then do Hook-ups. After doing either Hook-ups or Tapping, the Stress Reduction process in Part 5 of Calibration should be appropriate in that the arm should stay up on each of the zip-ups and go down on the zip-down.

PART 6. *"YES"/"NO" RESPONSE:*

Have your partner say the following statement to you and then muscle check you:

- "Your body will demonstrate a 'Yes' response." (Your arm should stay up.)
- "Your body will demonstrate a 'No' response." (Your arm should go down.)

By having completed Calibration you should get appropriate responses to both of these questions—switched-on for the "yes" and switched-off for the "no."

APPENDIX B

Executive Summary
A Revolution in Training:
The Bottom Line Results of
The Switched-On Selling Seminar

A Research Study With 695 Salespeople

BY

DR. JERRY V. TEPLITZ

Jerry Teplitz Enterprises, Inc
1304 Woodhurst Drive
Virginia Beach, VA 23454
800 – 77-RELAX or 757 496-8008
FAX 757 496-9955
Email - Jerry@Teplitz.com
www.Teplitz.com

The following is the Executive Summary of the results of the research study Jerry conducted with 695 salespeople to show the power and effectiveness of the Switched-On Courses to yield powerful results.

Executive Summary

The Switched-On Selling (SOS) seminar was designed to allow participants to overcome their fears so that they can become successful salespeople. The SOS seminar is revolutionary because it does not teach any sales techniques. Rather, it teaches participants how to determine which areas of the selling process are causing him or her stress and difficulty. Then participants learn how to use movement exercises called Brain Gyms® to re-wire their brains so that they are able to adapt to new opportunities and changes.

This report presents the updating of an analysis conducted in 2001, when data from 365 participants' pre- and post-seminar questionnaires was compared to 61 participants who completed and returned the One-Month questionnaire. An analysis was conducted on all eighteen questions as well as on the Overall Response Total for all eighteen questions.

The updated group added data from 330 salespeople to the data in the original study, which provided data for a total of 695 participants. This group was compared to a group of 124 respondents who completed the questionnaire one month after the seminar.

Switched-On Networking seminar participants completed a self-assessment questionnaire before the seminar began, immediately after the seminar, and one month after attending the seminar. The responses to the initial questionnaire indicated how the participants viewed themselves in relationship to the selling process. Participants' responses to the questionnaire immediately after the seminar indicated whether the materials presented in the seminar changed their perceptions of themselves. Administering the questionnaire one month after the seminar determined whether the changes indicated on the second questionnaire were genuine and if they held.

The analysis shows that participants' self-perception of their sales ability improved dramatically at the end of the seminar. The analysis also shows that participant's positive perceptions about their sales abilities improved even further when they were back in the field selling.

This report also presents the results of an insurance company study that shows how the SOS seminar affects salespeople's bottom line. One team of salespeople in the company attended the seminar and another group did not. Salespeople who attended the SOS seminar increased sales 39 percent over those who did not attend the seminar. In addition, the group that attended the seminar increased their premium levels 71 percent over those who did not attend the seminar.

Finally, a pest control company put half of their sales force through the SOS seminar in June 2009, which was during the middle of the recession and the other half through it in October 2009 during the slow recovery. Attendees were tracked for one year. In that one year period one sales person had a 300 percent increase in sales. Company profits doubled and the company was the number one distributor on two of the company's high end product lines.

To read the entire Switched-On Selling Research Report, you can go to www.Teplitz.com/BrainGymResearch.html

APPENDIX C

Executive Summaries from Other Research

Following are Executive Summaries of other research studies conducted by Dr. Teplitz on the impact of other Switched-On training seminars. To read each report in its entirety, go to www.Teplitz.com/BrainGymResearch.html

Switched-On Selling Seminar Research for Bankers Report

People going into banking don't usually view themselves as salespeople. When they are put into positions where they have to sell, many quickly discover the challenges of selling. While they can read books, attend seminars, watch DVDs, and listen to CDs to learn sales techniques, only a few achieve the highest levels of sales success. Until now...

Our study indicates that powerful changes occurred for 87 participants from five banks who had attended the one-day Switched-On Networking seminar (SOS). Each seminar was conducted at different times and locations. Another more in-depth study of 695 salespeople from all types of sales positions achieved very similar results.

Using self-evaluation forms that were completed by the participants at the beginning and at the end of the seminar, our study showed that a banker's self-perception of his or her sales ability improved very dramatically by the end of the SOS seminar. A number of the participants also completed a third self-evaluation form one month later. Reviewing that data showed even further improvement once the participants were back on the job at their banks.

Switched-On Network Marketing Seminar
Research Report

The Switched-On Network Marketing (SONM) seminar is for people who are involved in network or multilevel marketing and it was designed to allow the participants to overcome their fears so that they can become successful network marketers.

This report presents the results of a seventeen-item self-assessment questionnaire that 95 SONM participants answered before the seminar, immediately after the seminar, and one month after the seminar. The analysis showed that participants experienced very positive outcomes and dramatically altered their view of themselves in relationship to the network marketing process by the end of the seminar. The results one month later found that the changes not only held but that they actually improved even further.

Switched-On Management Seminar
Research Report

The Switched-On Management (SOM) seminar is a practical self-development management training program for managers to create a more successful, effective, and dynamic company or organization. SOM is designed to help managers become more effective with management skills they have and develop skills in new areas of management.

This report presents the results of a pilot study conducted on the impact of the SOM seminar. For this study, 21 SOM participants completed a self-assessment questionnaire before the seminar began and again at the end of the seminar. The questionnaire that participants completed at the beginning of the seminar provided a baseline measurement of how the they viewed themselves in relationship to the various parts of the management process. The questionnaire that participants completed at the end of the seminar indicated whether the seminar had changed their perception of themselves.

The responses to pre- and post-seminar questionnaires indicate that seminar participants' self-perception of their management ability increased significantly at the conclusion of the seminar.

To read all of the above research studies, go to
www.Teplitz.com/BrainGymResearch.html

Brain Gym Annotated Research Chronology

The Brain Gym Foundation has posted on its Web site a research report summarizing twenty-plus years of Brain Gym research.

To read the complete report, go to
www.BrainGym.org

ACKNOWLEDGEMENTS

Donna Fisher:

Birthing a book is a process requiring dedication, commitment, support, and vision. And I am grateful for my network of support and in particular my partners in writing this book for providing all of those factors throughout this process.

Thank you, Jerry, for our many years as master-mind buddies supporting each other personally and professionally. I am honored and grateful for the opportunity to collaborate with you and share your Brain Gym expertise so that people can take their networking to a new level of ease, fun, and effectiveness. I acknowledge you for being a thought leader regarding brain dynamics and how to align our body and minds to live true to our hearts and spirits. I acknowledge you for your commitment and vision to have Brain Gym processes easily available for people to enhance their lives in all arenas.

Thank you, Norma Eckroate, for your talent as a writer and your loving, fun spirit! Working with you has made this one of the most fun book projects I have done so far! I appreciate how our working relationship so easily and naturally evolved into a heart-centered, fun, supportive friendship! I appreciate your talent and dedication to reviewing this material so thoroughly to make it easily understandable, useable, and beneficial to our readers.

I appreciate Robert Tennyson Stevens for inspiring me to upgrade my language and speak heart-felt words of empowerment and how doing so has enhanced my networking effectiveness and my life. I appreciate everyone who has read any of my books or attended any of my programs for providing the impetus for me to continue to appreciate and share the value of people connecting and creating opportunities through the networking process. Special thanks to everyone who provided examples, success stories, feedback, and testimonials for *Switched-On Networking.*

Dr. Jerry V. Teplitz:

I'd like to thank Dr. John Diamond from whom I learned Behavioral Kinesiology, which became a stepping stone to so much of my work. I am also extremely grateful to Dr. Paul Dennison and Gail Dennison, creators of Brain Gym, for their willingness to allow me to use their materials to develop a seminar called Switched-On Selling in 1986 and for their willingness to write and publish the *Brain Gym for Business* book with me. Since then, the Switched-On Selling seminar evolved into two additional seminars, Switched-On Network Marketing and Switched-On Management. And this book is now the third in our *Switched-On* book series, which also include *Switched-On Selling* and *Switched-On Living.*

I am grateful to Donna Fisher, one of the top networking experts in the country who is the author of a number of books on the subject. I've known Donna for many years and have been in a master-mind group with her for a long time. I greatly appreciate the wisdom and masterful strategies on Networking that she has brought to this collaboration.

This book, like the others, would simply not have happened if Norma Eckroate had not been willing to become part of it and stick with it over the proverbial bumps in the road. Both Donna and I really appreciate her skills that make this book possible. Thank you, Norma!

In the production of this book I'd like to thank the following people who played crucial roles: Daniel Yaeger for his wonderful cover artwork; Lynn Synder King for the excellent design and layout; Cris Arbo for her great drawings; Beth Agresta and Richard Hagen, and Elizabeth Balcar for their photographs; and Elizabeth Balcar for photoshopping the photos, which was an enormous job.

BIOGRAPHIES

DONNA FISHER

Donna Fisher is a recognized expert on the topics of networking, communication, and business development. She loves being a catalyst for people to expand their thinking to new ideas and new possibilities.

After earning her degree in Business Administration from Appalachian State University, Donna worked in the regional accounting center for Exxon Corporation. Leaving there because she desired a career path that was more people oriented, she took a position as a marketing rep for McDonnell Douglas Automation where she quickly advanced to senior marketing rep.

But Donna's heart was still calling her to do something even more people oriented when she gladly accepted a position at a nonprofit organization, The Center for Attitudinal Healing in Houston, Texas. She became the Executive Director of the Center which is where she says she learned "how to network"—because in the non-profit industry you are consistently networking throughout your community for support and donations. Part of Donna's job at the Center was training the volunteers and speaking to groups and organizations about the center's mission, leading to the discovery of her love of both speaking and training.

In 1989 Donna began speaking to groups, organizations, and companies about the power of attitude, communication skills, networking, and personal accountability. She became a member of the National Speakers Association, where she has earned the Certified Speaking Professional (CSP) designation. Donna is the author of *Power Networking, People Power, Power Networking Nuggets* and *Professional Networking for Dummies,* which are often used as reference books in companies and universities. She also co-authored *Power NetWeaving* with Bob Littell, founder of NetWeavers International.

Donna is a Certified Instructor for Mastery Systems' program "Language of Mastery," where she teaches the principles of "Conscious Language™" and how to create new life experiences through your speaking.

Donna is truly an entrepreneur at heart. She loves to create and grow fun and profitable businesses—and teach others how to do the same. Her other businesses include the Percussion Center, a music store, specializing in drums and percussion, where she has grown the business 35 percent since 2001. She has also created a line of crocheted shawls, wraps, and fiber wall hangings called Soft & Luxurious.

Donna loves coming up with and implementing new ideas—ideas for starting a business, growing a business, and creating new possibilities in all areas of life.

Contact Information for Donna Fisher:
- Books, Trainings, Presentations - Website: www.DonnaFisher.com; Phone: 713-789-2484, email: Donna@DonnaFisher.com
- Networking with Kindness Campaign - Website: www.NetworkingWithKindness.com
- Virtual Networking Events and Power Networking Webinars - Website: www.NetworkingJam.com and www.TheMingleGroup.com

DR. JERRY V. TEPLITZ

Dr. Jerry V. Teplitz's background is as unique as the techniques and approaches he teaches. He is a graduate of Hunter College and Northwestern University School of Law and practiced as an attorney for the Illinois Environmental Protection Agency.

Jerry's career took a dramatic change of direction when he received Masters and Doctorate Degrees in Wholistic Health Sciences from Columbia Pacific University. He was on the faculty of the U.S. Chamber of Commerce Institute for Organization Management for nine years.

In the association industry, Dr. Teplitz' expertise has been recognized by speaking engagements at such prestigious organizations as the American Society of Association Executives (ASAE) Great Ideas Conference and ASAE's Annual Convention, the Professional Convention Management Association Annual Convention, where the feedback was so positive that Dr. Teplitz was selected to be a Best-in-Class Speaker, and the Canadian Society of Association Executives Annual Convention, where he was selected as an Association Excellence Speaker.

Dr. Teplitz was a field manager for the Inscape Publishing Company for thirty years and he has been president of his own speaking and consulting firm for over thirty-seven years. Jerry conducts seminars in the areas of leadership training, stress management, and sales development.

The list of clients Dr. Teplitz has spoken to and consulted for includes such organizations as IBM, Motorola, FDIC, and Time, Inc. In addition, he has spoken to Century 21, Holiday Inns, International Management Council, Young Presidents' Organization, Associated General Contractors, GlaxoSmithKline, American Bankers Association, plus over four hundred colleges and universities across the United States and Canada.

Dr. Teplitz has been a Brain Gym 101 Instructor since 1986. He served on the Brain Gym International Board of Directors for nine years and chaired the Brain Gym Marketing Committee. Jerry is the creator of the *Switched-On Selling, Management,* and *Network Marketing* Seminars and Instructor Certification training programs. He also assisted in the original development of the *Switched-On Golf* Seminar and is certified to teach it.

Jerry is the author of *Managing Your Stress In Difficult Times: Succeeding In Times of Change,* the #1 Amazon Best Seller *Switched-On Selling: Balance Your Brain for Sales Success* and *Switched-On Living.* He co-authored *Brain Gym for Business* with the founders of Brain Gym, Dr. Paul Dennison and Gail Dennison. Articles on Jerry have appeared in such publications as *Successful Meetings, Prevention,* and *Travel and Leisure Golf* magazines. He has also been listed in several editions of Who's Who in America.

As a professional speaker, he has spoken to over one million people. Dr. Teplitz has also been honored by his peers in the National Speakers Association by earning the title of Certified Speaking Professional. Finally, he is host of his internet radio talk show, Healthy Alternatives on www.WebTalkRadio.net.

Contact information for Dr. Jerry Teplitz:
- Dr. Jerry's products: Website: www.Teplitz.com/Catalog
- Keynote speeches and seminars: 1-757-496-8008; Email: Info@Teplitz.com
- Switched-On Selling seminar and instructor training: Website: www.Teplitz.com/switched-main

NORMA ECKROATE

Norma Eckroate has a doctorate in holistic life counseling from the University of Sedona. She teaches law of attraction, metaphysics, and spirituality and is a licensed spiritual practitioner at the Agape International Spiritual Center. Norma is a regular guest contributor on Andrea Sholer's "Real Life LoA (Law of Attraction)" on Blog Talk Radio.

Norma coauthored the books *Switched-on Selling* and *Switched-On Living* with stress management expert Jerry V. Teplitz, Ph.D. She has also coauthored books with experts on topics that range from holistic health for animals to positive dog training and Santa Claus. Her recent titles include The Natural Cat (revised edition); *The Dog Whisperer, The Puppy Whisperer; The Dog Whisperer Presents Good Habits for Great Dogs,* and *The Santa Story Revisited: How to Give Your Children a Santa They Will Never Outgrow.*

Norma is currently writing a book on weight loss, emotional healing, and the Law of Attraction.

Contact information for Norma Eckroate:
- Weight Loss and Law of Attraction
  Website: www.NaturalWeightLossMagic.com
- *Dog Whisperer* books, DVDs and free advice featuring
  Paul Owens, the "Original" Dog Whisperer:
  Website: www.DogWhispererDVD.com
- *The Natural Cat:* Website: www.TheNaturalCat.net
- *The Santa Story Revisited:* Website: www.TheSantaStory.com

Brain Gym Movements and Exercises

Quick Reference Guide

INDEX

A

Products from Dr. Jerry V. Teplitz

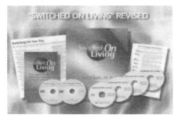

Switched-On Living®
The Complete Learning System

Price: $ 299.⁰⁰

- 2 DVD Seminar Videos
- 4 CD Audio Programs
- 2 Wall Charts
- Quick Reminder Wallet Card
- Switched-On Living—The Book

Developed by Dr. Teplitz, the **Switched-On Living®** Personal Energy Program teaches you innovative techniques for achieving peak performance and optimum well-being. A complete package which will empower your life in so many ways!

POPULAR

DVD: Creating High Energy Websites & PR Materials

The energy can make or break the sale. Without even realizing it, your viewers are immediately affected by the energy in your marketing materials or web site, and ultimately this will cause them to read on, or back out..

Price: $ 149.⁹⁷

Many world class companies *will not put out a product until it has been muscle checked,* using the same techniques provided in Dr. Teplitz' DVD.

In fact, Jack Canfield, co-author of the **"Chicken Soup for the Soul"** book series, has publicly stated "we won't release a single *Chicken Soup* product until it's gone through the process developed by Dr. Teplitz, to make certain it is high energy!"

Products from Dr. Jerry V. Teplitz

Book: Managing Stress in Difficult Times
$ 18.⁰⁰

From a ninety-second cure for headaches, to five minute relief from a migraine, to technique that immediately raise your energy, this fully illustrated book offers hands-on, proven methods to immediately manage stress.

Book: Brain Gym for Business
$ 18.⁰⁰

This book should be in every office in America. It offers a series of simple exercises called Brain Gym, designed to minimize stress in the work environment. Divided by job positions, this provides instant boosters for on-the-job success.

Power of the Mind DVD
$ 95.⁰⁰

Unleash the power of your mind! Learn how to tap into the energy coming from your mind; how you can control it, direct it and use it to achieve what you want in your life.

IDEAL-WEIGHT (Subliminal Music CD) Steven Halpern
$ 20.⁰⁰

Beautiful, relaxing music plus subliminal suggestions let you listen & grow thinner! Specially composed music has helped many listeners achieve the results they seek!

Leadership Power to New Levels of Excellence DVD
$ 95.⁰⁰

This DVD Seminar shows you how to take your leadership abilities to the highest levels and provides instant techniques for managing your business and environment.

Accelerating Learning (Subliminal Music CD) Steven Halpern
$ 20.⁰⁰

Reduce stress, improve concentration & stay in "the zone" for optimal learning! Subliminal suggestions harness the power of your subconscious mind, and Halpern's Non-Predictive Music™ creates breakthroughs for 'students' of all ages.

Par and Beyond: Secrets to Better Golf DVD
$ 95.⁰⁰

Dramatically cut your handicap ! Golf abilities, like everything we learn, are literally controlled by neuron connections in the brain. This program directly and immediately strengthens these connections & will teach you a 15-point breakthrough system to put your game over the top Includes a handy wallet card to carry with you on the links!

For Digital Download Versions of these products, visit the website www.teplitz.com/Catalog.html

100% Satisfaction

All products come with a 60-Day Money-Back Guarantee.